The Archi+ec+ure

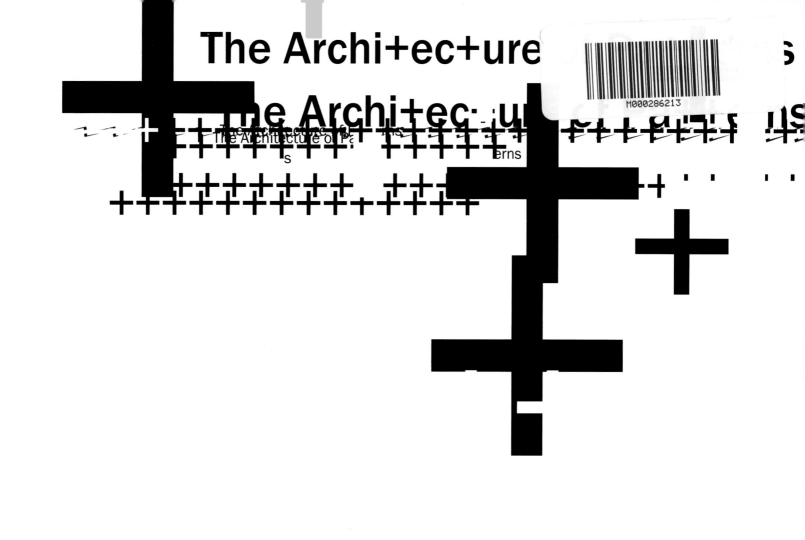

The Archi+ec+ure

The Architecture of Pa

erns

M000286213

THE ARCHITECTURE OF PATTERNS

FOREWORD BY SANFORD KWINTER

PAUL ANDERSEN + DAVID SALOMON

W. W. NORTON & COMPANY   NEW YORK • LONDON

Art direction and graphic design: David Carson (dcarson@earthlink.net)
Assistant graphic designer: Kati Shaw

Printed in Singapore
First Edition

For information about permission to reproduce selections from
this book, write to Permissions, W. W. Norton & Company, Inc.,
500 Fifth Avenue, New York, NY 10110

For information about special discounts for bulk purchases,
please contact W. W. Norton Special Sales at
specialsales@wwnorton.com or 800-233-4830

Manufacturing by KHL
Production manager: Leeann Graham

Library of Congress Cataloging-in-Publication Data

Andersen, Paul, 1975–
    The architecture of patterns / Paul Andersen, David L.
Salomon ; foreword by Sanford Kwinter. — 1st ed.
        p.   cm.
        Includes bibliographical references and index.
        ISBN 978-0-393-73293-1 (pbk.)
        1. Architecture—Composition, proportion, etc.
    2. Architectural design. I. Salomon, David L. II. Title.

NA2760.A53 2010
720—dc22   2010009293

ISBN: 978-0-393-73293-1 (pbk.)

W. W. Norton & Company, Inc., 500 Fifth Avenue,
New York, N.Y. 10110
www.wwnorton.com
W. W. Norton & Company Ltd., Castle House,
75/76 Wells Street, London W1T 3QT

0 9 8 7 6 5 4 3 2 1

CONTENTS

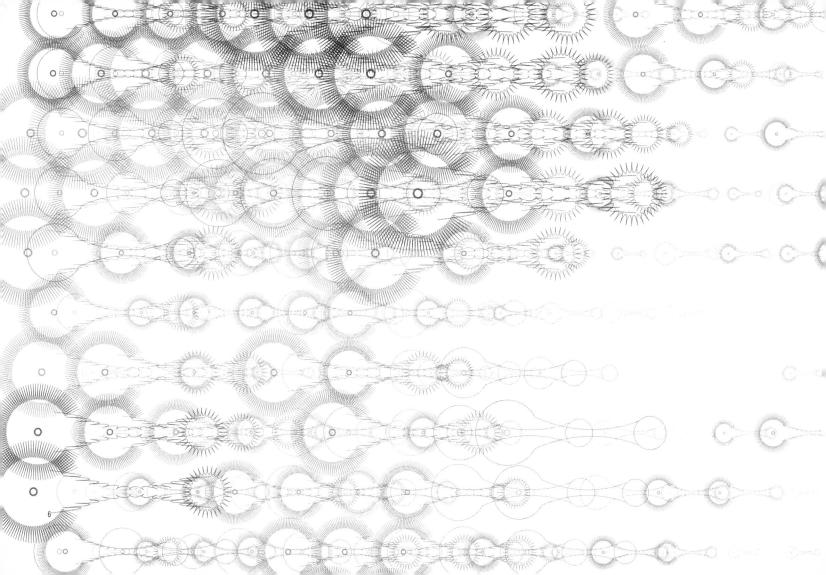

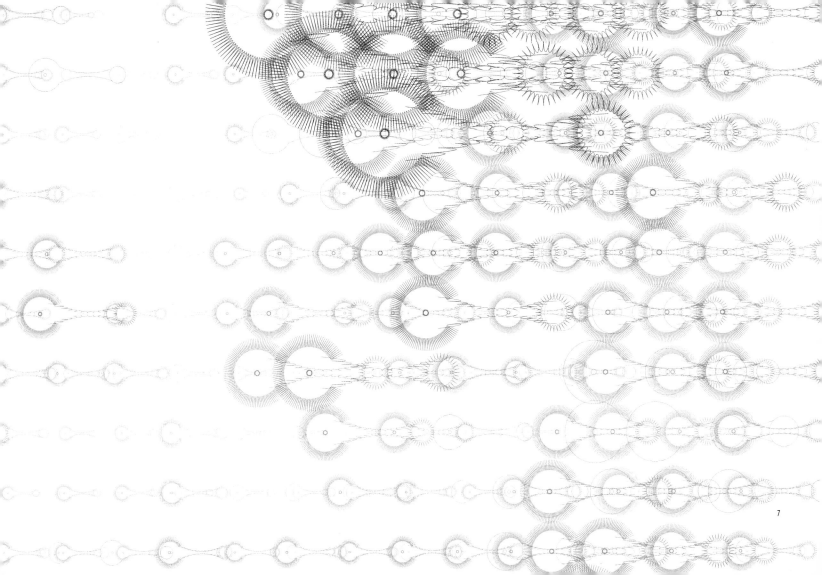

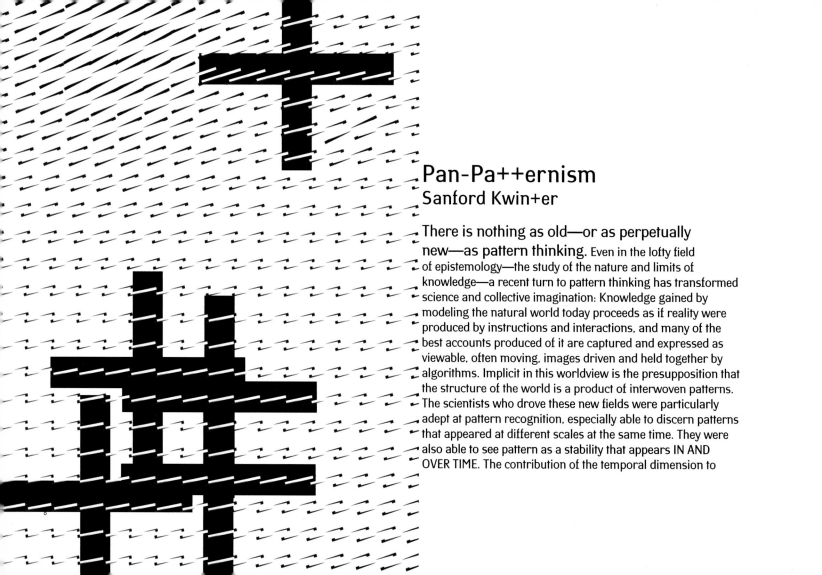

Pan-Pa++ernism
Sanford Kwin+er

There is nothing as old—or as perpetually new—as pattern thinking. Even in the lofty field of epistemology—the study of the nature and limits of knowledge—a recent turn to pattern thinking has transformed science and collective imagination: Knowledge gained by modeling the natural world today proceeds as if reality were produced by instructions and interactions, and many of the best accounts produced of it are captured and expressed as viewable, often moving, images driven and held together by algorithms. Implicit in this worldview is the presupposition that the structure of the world is a product of interwoven patterns. The scientists who drove these new fields were particularly adept at pattern recognition, especially able to discern patterns that appeared at different scales at the same time. They were also able to see pattern as a stability that appears IN AND OVER TIME. The contribution of the temporal dimension to our expanded understanding of order transformed our general approach to shape itself, in effect returning us to the most primitive, and one of the most powerful, aspects of our biological endowment, our capacity to read and harvest order in our environment for purposes of survival. All of life, in the evolutionary sense, is a hunt for pattern as well as for the means to discern it. Both the nervous and the semiological system of both predator and the prey (predation includes the act of ingesting or combusting any part of the environment, vegetative, mineral, informational, or carnal) are programs to communicate—to send and receive— as well as to stabilize the environment, via pattern.

The sciences of pattern today are hence through and through ecological ones. But the ecologies they presuppose are unexpected and complex. We know through the work of many neurologists how geometric patterns are generated in the brain by "pathological" agents: as part of the stages of sleep, by lesions, migraine, even by applying pressure to the eyeballs. It is as if geometry provided a necessary, invisible scaffold for perceptual experience and is forced out of hiding only under certain aggravated conditions. Similarly, as the authors note in their text, cybernetic anthropologist Gregory Bateson militated for the inclusion of "noise" into

our accounts of the functioning of communicative and ecological webs. Noise is almost never extraneous, and in fact is largely viewable as bearing a pattern that has not yet been discerned. Later, hard science discovered manifold versions of this phenomenon, such as the patterns described by "one-over-f" systems ("brown" or "pink" noise) whose structure—almost universal— is a prerequisite for the production of novel and ever more efficient and responsive patterns. In yet another context, the metallurgist Cyril Stanley Smith identified the "imperfections" in material lattices and substructural orders as the real site of functional pattern, the place where regular material behaviors find their source. In each case, the management and exploitation of trans-scalar relationships of pattern is the source of structural "performance."

David Carson, the designer of the book you now hold in your hands, long ago showed how noise, introduced into the typographic signal system in the form of interferences, deletions, "defective transcriptions," and other versions of "distress," actually provoked the activation of pattern-recognition responses in readers that previously remained only latent. For a "5" to be read as an "S" and for a "4" to be recognized as itself despite the deletion of every mark endemic to it aside from the left vertex whose position is fully unique to that letterform (it is different from that of the uppercase "A" and yet invokes it), it is necessary to call up levels of "approximative competence" and a heavily reinforced computation of the larger typographic and signifying environment or relational context. One might say that this state represents the moment when reading approximates the heat and dynamics of the primordial hunt, the intensive focus required to detect part-forms and part-movements by elaborating them algorithmically in one's head. When the just word is discovered, it is in effect stabilized but is also captured and ingested.

The human story—the story that resists the deformations of both rationality and science and yet represents a tolerable "revolution" within science and rational knowledge each time it makes its periodic return into these domains—is the story of pattern. Pattern in the modern era (the present) is often represented as the "qualitative" (and hence the "poor") component in the knowledge world. In many ways, however, this represents a signal mistake in thinking that today's ostensible pattern revival implicitly seeks to correct: pattern is the means through which the world at once communicates and materially interacts with itself. Pattern is at once the empirical and the abstract.

No other notion or mathematical object embraces the two domains at once. I would suggest that in this it would not be entirely farfetched to see a revival of a certain Spinozism in our midst: Pattern (like Spinoza's "Nature") appears as the one Substance whose two inseparable Attributes are, on the one hand, MATTER and on the other, THOUGHT.

With this hypothesis in mind, I believe one will more easily access the deeper intentions and implications of this provocative book and see in the very approach to pattern itself and especially in its capacity to dissolve and resolve opposition, paradox, and the persistent fallacy of irreducible essences, a new approach to form—FORM AS ENVIRONMENT—as well as a new and rich design method that constitutes a necessary radical hypothesis for our ecological future, that of a new Pantheism itself.

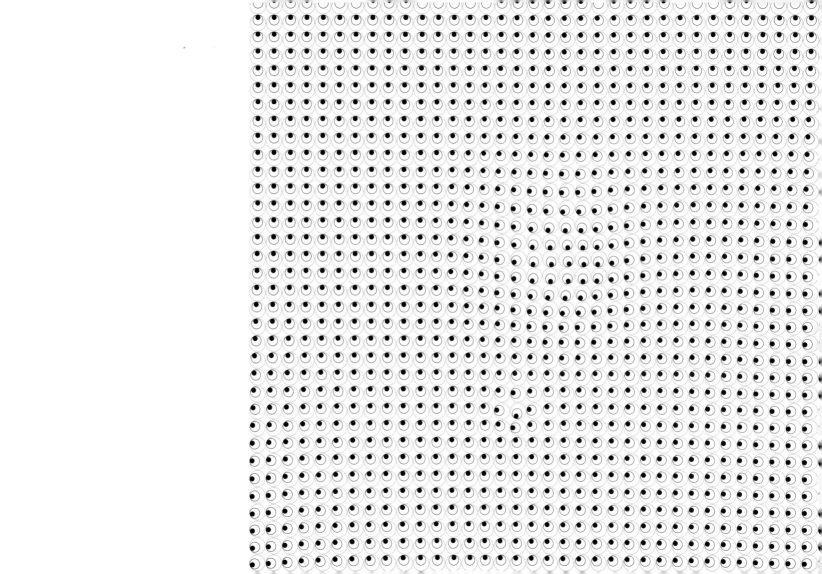

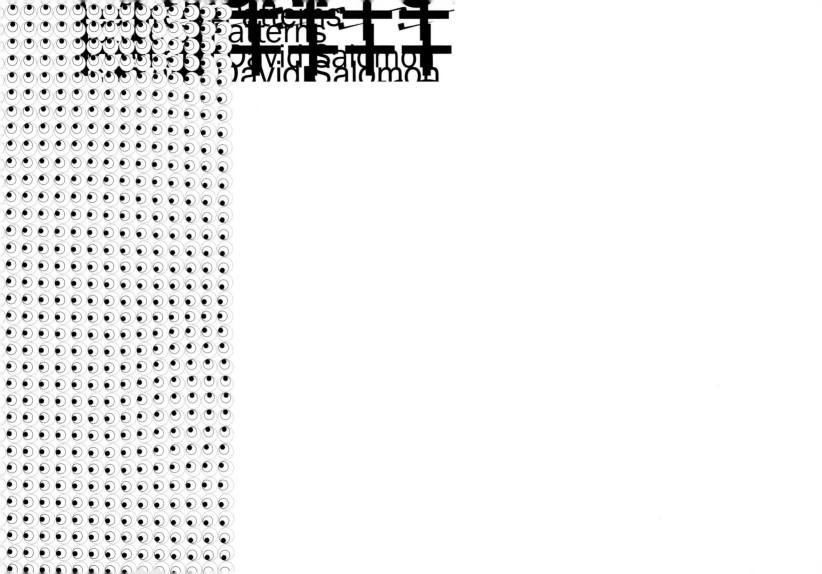

CHAPTER 1 : THE POWER OF THE GENERALIST

Of course, our failures are a consequence of many factors, but possibly one of the most important is the fact that society operates on the theory that specialization is the key to success, not realizing that specialization precludes comprehensive thinking.

R. Buckminster Fuller

On a Sunday morning in 1971, Bill Bowerman initiated a decades-long design evolution with his invention of the waffle sole, a project that merged three seemingly unrelated household objects. Seeing new possibilities for speed in a tire, a kitchen scale, and a waffle iron, he fabricated the first edition of the lightweight Moon Shoe, which yielded immediate results at the Munich marathon trials and helped launch Nike. His ability to generate novelty from a heterogeneous combination of sources is a particular form of intelligence—one that architecture shares in its most sophisticated state.

Bowerman's synthetic ingenuity was both facilitated by and embodied in a pattern, a regular grid of rubber pads whose development can be traced to the latest running shoes. A look at the soles of today's Nikes reveals that what started as uniform and functional, like many architectural patterns of its time, is now differentiated and multifarious. Advanced patterns in contemporary design are a confluence of diverse materials, performance requirements, environmental factors, aesthetic sensibilities, elastic geometries, and kinetic forces. But not all patterns are created equal.

The dramatic varieties present in contemporary buildings—in structural systems, facade compositions, circulation diagrams, wallpaper and textiles, urban designs, and even landscapes—typically perform either an aesthetic or a functional role, seldom both, and are rigid, stable, and homogenously repetitive. So while they have reinvigorated certain aspects of architecture, their full potential as dynamic agents of synthesis and multiplicity is only rarely fulfilled.

A refined view of patterns, one in which they are highly calibrated and elastic design primitives, can help architects perform a long-standing and neglected disciplinary role: integrating sensory, organizational, operational, structural, and environmental domains in a complex entity. Today, architecture is required to be precise and multivalent at the same time—for example, to be at once efficient and intricate, to generate complex programmatic solutions and an advanced formal sensibility, or to be both iconic and invisible. Patterns are able to synthesize these typically divergent demands because they operate simultaneously on abstract and physical registers. Functioning as both process and image, graphic and code, they are able to foreground the sensual while shaping matter and behavior by stealth. Tapping into their ability to migrate across genres (graphic patterns to structural to behavioral to thermal) and incorporate ideas from diverse sources situates

Nike Oregon Waffle (1973) and *Air Max 360 II* (2008). The regular pattern and uniform rubber construction of Bill Bowerman's historic waffle sole have given way to integrated patterns of plastics, gels, foams, and rubbers in a variety of colors. While the simplicity of the original grid is still present, its geometry and material composition have become more elaborate to boost the shoe's athletic and aesthetic performance.

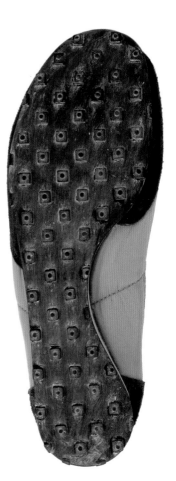

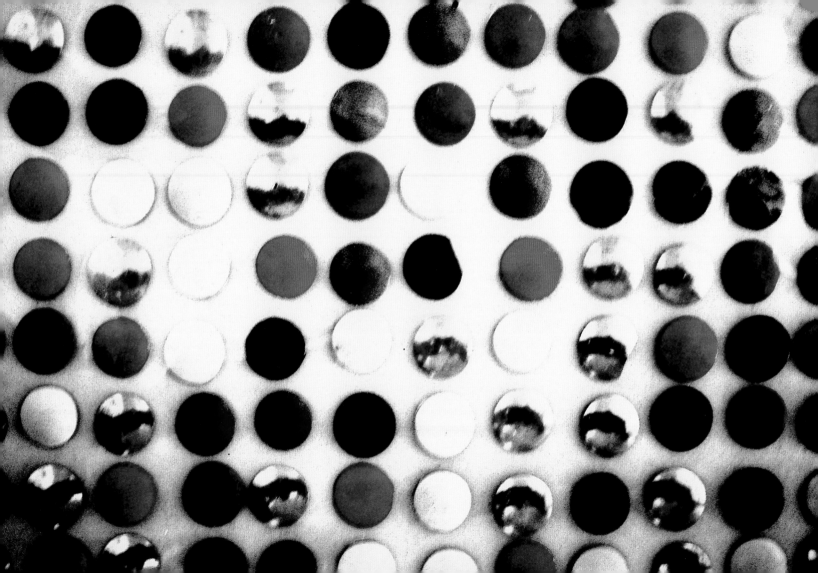

architects where they have always claimed to be, namely, at the intersection of the arts and the sciences.

In contrast to the isolationist logics and fragmented aesthetics of modernism and postmodernism, respectively, a new breed of multidimensional and synthetic patterns maneuver on spectra between organization and sensation, constancy and randomness, stability and flexibility, efficiency and extravagance, permanence and transience—with no clear predilection for the extremes. This redefinition of patterns means that their sensory, fleeting, and iterative traits are taken as seriously as their functional, everlasting, and essential ones—producing projects of protean vitality and multifarious intelligence.

Ubiquitous and Untheorized

Despite their popularity, the recent resurgence of patterns remains untheorized and their capabilities underutilized. No account of their proliferation has been given, nor have their increased morphological and functional capacities been thoroughly examined. In fact, the relationship between patterns and architecture hasn't been addressed in almost 30 years. So why the silence on patterns? There are a number of reasons: first, dissatisfaction with previous architectural conceptions of them; second, their everyday association with superficiality and planned obsolescence; third, the ambiguity of the term pattern; and fourth, the uncritical and one-dimensional use of them in design.

In scientific discourse, patterns are frequently synonymous with fundamental laws that govern physical reality; they serve as evidence of the general order of things behind the apparent chaos of the world. Similarly, a conception of patterns as ideal, unchanging, and reproducible design principles was promoted by the architectural theorist Christopher Alexander, who has dominated discourse on the subject for three decades. His patterns are presented as spatial, formal, and functional "truths" that are both observable in every "good design" and radically deterministic. While his theories have catalyzed contentious research methodologies in fields as diverse as computer science and sociology, in architectural discourse there has been relatively little controversy. Until now, architects have accepted his principles, used their universal and conservative nature to dismiss patterns entirely, or simply ignored the topic. By tapping into their newly developed potential to be elastic and specific, architects can reclaim them from Alexander without negating their organizational possibilities.

In contrast to Alexander's universal principles, patterns colloquially are seen as superficial images or cultural trends in the decorative and popular arts, realms in which they are more visually oriented and capricious. Resistance to patterns is often linked to a prejudice against shallowness and ephemerality. Architecture has a reputation of being durable—it is conventionally too slow, too stable, and too important to be fleeting—and thus patterns are condemned for failing to have any functional or long-term influence.

Multifunctional Diagrid

Paradoxically rejected for being alternatively timeless and too timely, deterministic and promiscuous, patterns are all too easily marginalized. It is no wonder that when the term is invoked, it loosely describes any temporal or spatial repetition of objects or behaviors. With no clear conceptual definitions, patterns are deployed with concomitant abandon in design and little sense of what exactly constitutes a pattern or why one is more relevant, capable, or desirable than the next. The tenuous theoretical and practical status of the pattern is enough to make any designer skeptical. However, instead of dismissing them, we hope to give authority to a new generation of patterns, ones that extend the best features of their predecessors and add some new swerves.

Temporally, patterns that never seem to go out of style can be hybridized with others that are meteoric, that are momentarily brilliant. Procedurally, a pattern can be defined as both an original and a copy; as an ideal or generalized model to be followed and its repetitive materialization. This can be seen in the world of clothing design, where "pattern" alternatively describes the die from which fabric is cut and also the decorative print or weave of the material that gets cut. No longer purely limited to static motifs or stable systems, today's varieties are imbued with elasticity, aperiodicity, opulence, variegation, and idiosyncrasy, qualities that allow them to combine novel organizational models and sensuous environments. Pliable enough to be customized and adapted to a project's numerous contingencies, **patterns undergo radical changes without losing their aesthetic identity.** Unlike their predecessors, a retheorized notion

Swiss Re Building, Foster and Associates, London (2004); *Seattle Central Library,* OMA (2004); *Prada Aoyama,*
Herzog and de Meuron (2003). Despite their divergent programs, forms, locations, and clients, these three projects
rely on the diagrid for structural stability and visual coherence.

of patterns as multistatic, multidimensional, and multifunctional provides architects with a device to connect apparently incongruent categories and synthesize a multitude of performances, project requirements, and informational types in a perception-based medium.

The expansive palette of pattern types suggests that they can make unexpected connections between wildly dissimilar territories, a capacity that speaks to the historical debate of specialization versus generalization. Since Vitruvius, architectural expertise has been controversially defined as an ability to synthesize ideas from other fields without a specific body of knowledge to call its own. Similarly, the need to generalize and organize information across different disciplines makes any claims regarding architecture's autonomy difficult, if not impossible. Despite the many modernist calls to specialize (in technology, formal invention, administration, etc.), architects' primary skills are connecting far-flung epistemological frontiers and identifying alternative trajectories of design evolution.

While many lament this state, the skills and talents of the generalist are very much in demand today. As society is ever more segmented along informational categories—and as design embraces new technologies, generates new modes of knowledge and assimilates new cultural norms—merging categorically distinct interests within complex objects and environments remains a difficult but essential task. However, today's version of the generalist should not be mistaken as a jack-of-all-trades or the "universal man." Rather, the talents demanded of the generalist today are opportunistic intuition and entrepreneurial know-how.

The Office of Metropolitan Architecture and its counterpart, AMO, have been playing the part of generalist for quite some time, providing architectural, urban, graphic, in-store information, and strategic

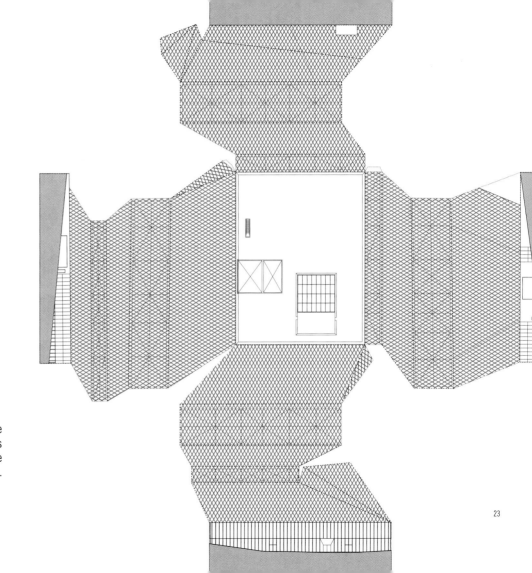

Seattle Central Library. Unfolded elevation. The diamond pattern of the building envelope is uniform regardless of where it occurs or how the interior behind it is programmed.

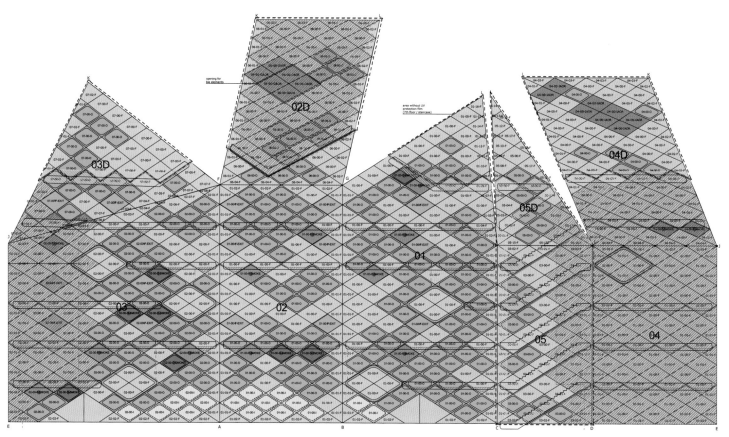

Prada Aoyama. Unfolded elevation. Although the diamonds' sizes are the same, panels contain different kinds of glass, vents, and openings depending on various functional requirements.

branding services, among others. Its design of the Seattle Central Library highlights the architects' agility in curating the talents of a variety of specialists—graphic designers, engineers, and interior designers, to name a few. But the envelope design also demonstrates the flexibility of patterns to simultaneously perform unrelated roles. Given the divergent nature of the various components and personalities present in the project, the diagrid pattern present on the exterior skin gathers together what would otherwise remain fragmented. In contrast to other formal and graphic devices used throughout the interior to make distinctions—for example, the indexical use of color and graphics to indicate circulation elements and programmatic spaces—the diagrid incorporates the project's idiosyncrasies into a coherent, if internally heterogeneous, object.

The diagrid envelope, which has regained popularity and evolved dramatically in recent years, exhibits similar geometric homogeneity in Foster's Swiss Re office tower and Herzog and de Meuron's Prada store in Aoyama. And as a result, it tends to be monoprogrammatic—to serve exclusively as a structural solution. Prada

Aoyama takes a step toward expanding the diagrid's role. Though the diamonds in the pattern are uniform, each is treated like a module, capable of containing a variety of materials, building systems, and effects. While appearing at first to be a purely aesthetic aspect of the design, on closer inspection the diagrid is a multisystem organizational device. The building's unfolded facade drawing indicates how the pattern influences the external structural lattice, internal

the pa++ern meets numerous functional demands with a graphically consistent solution

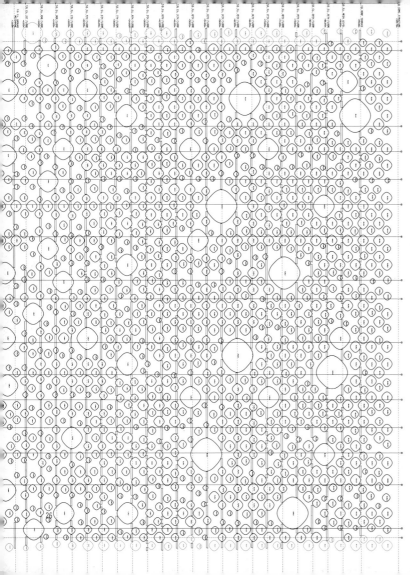

(opposite) *O-14*. Model detail. The typically uniform, sharp, diamond shaped openings in the diagrid are differentiated and rounded to create a spotted appearance.

O-14, Reiser + Umemoto, Dubai, UAE (2007). Unfolded elevation. A differentiated diagrid establishes the building's aesthetic identity and also establishes reflexive relationships between material, structural, environmental, and optical effects.

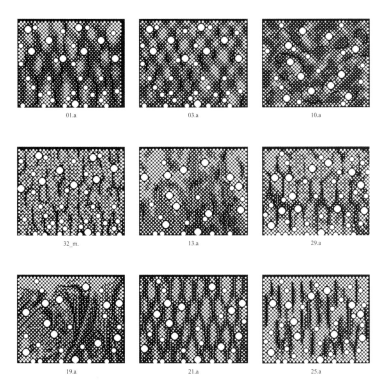

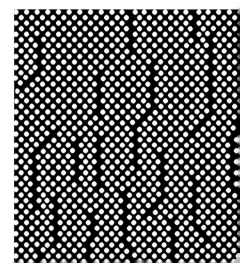

01.a 03.a 10.a

32_m. 13.a 29.a

19.a 21.a 25.a

O-14. Shell development. Variations of the diagrid pattern yield a range of visual effects.

a type of static motion perhaps?

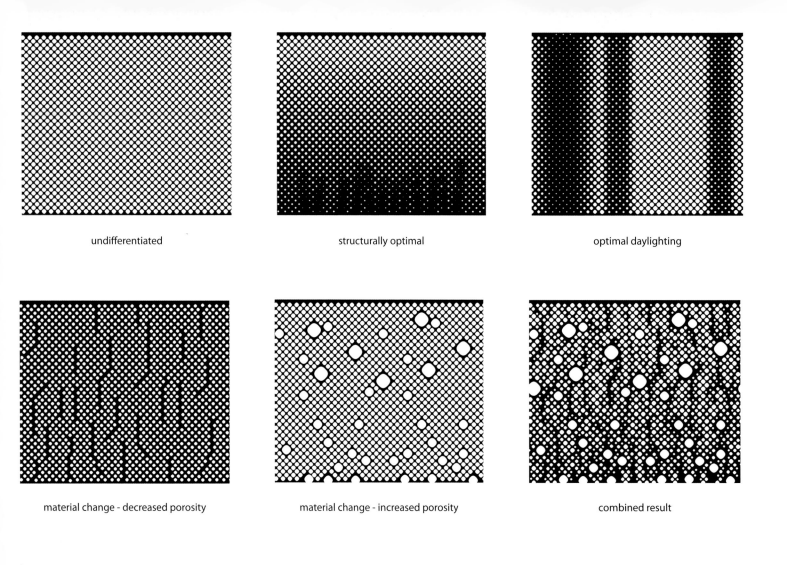

undifferentiated

structurally optimal

optimal daylighting

material change - decreased porosity

material change - increased porosity

combined result

O-14. Construction photographs. The building was cast in place with reusable foam plugs in four different sizes.

(opposite) *O-14*. Shell analysis. A structural diagram of the unfolded facade indicates the size of vertical loads, which progressively increase from top to bottom despite the relatively homogenous distribution of apertures in the envelope.

partitions, the distribution of glazing types, massing, and slab and stair placements. Unlike the Swiss Re building in London—where the diagrid acts in a solely structural manner and its presence is suppressed by the spiraling stripes of the curtain wall—at Aoyama, even more so than at Seattle, the pattern meets numerous functional demands with a graphically consistent solution. Yet, in all three cases, the inelastic nature of the diagrid prevents it from performing (either structurally or visually) as both a generic and a specific solution, a capability that is characteristic of more complex patterns.

When the same pattern that generates a building's visual, formal, or spatial sensibility—for example, a floral or hexagonal one—concurrently serves as an effective delivery device for informational, climatic, structural, and other programmatic services, unconventional architectural categories and methods emerge, new hierarchies are established, and boundaries are perforated. The deployment of dramatic and multifunctional patterns suggests that architects can use their prodigious (and currently maligned) formal dexterity to mold various sensory fields and reshape even the most mundane building systems.

O-14. Model.

pattern is a great way to meet many needs at once. It speaks multiple languages

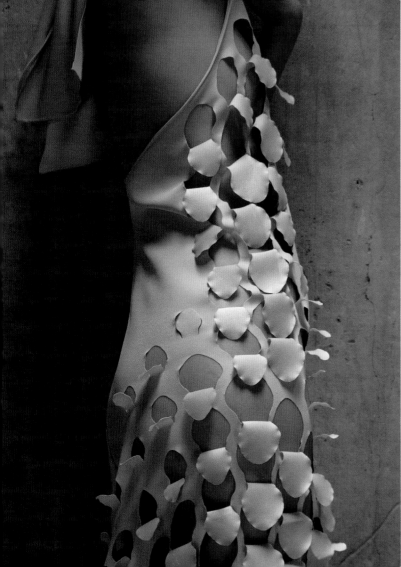

Elastic Diagrid

Given this dual capacity, there are two equally relevant (if seemingly paradoxical) ways to take advantage of patterns' multifunctional capabilities: begin a design project with a chosen pattern and adapt it to meet specific goals, or identify patterns native to the problem at hand and use them as diagrams for design. In either case, **design begins with patterns.** Instead of form following function, patterns produce performances.

A pattern's pliability enables an architect to establish some relevance up front—selecting a diagrid privileges structural sensibilities, while a Miuccia Prada print would be more culturally charged—and, by loading it with additional demands and desires, to increase its specificity. Diversity and novelty can be bred either by repeating a pattern and simultaneously differentiating it in response to variable contingencies (adaptation) or by patterning standard, mass-produced materials, building systems, or types (customization). In all cases, it is the ability of patterns to distort, absorb, amplify, and fluctuate that makes such differentiation possible.

Clad Cuts Dress (Spring/Summer 2005), Atelier Manferdini.

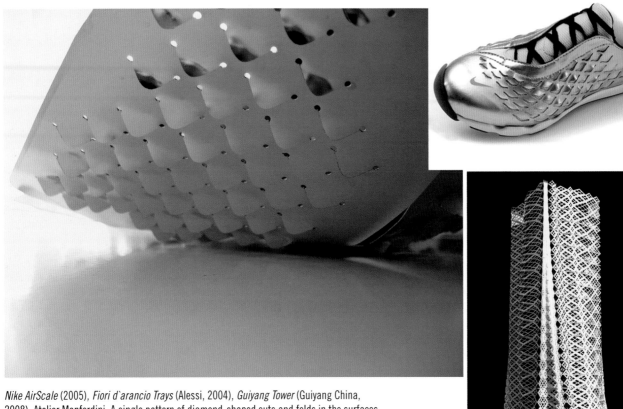

Nike AirScale (2005), *Fiori d'arancio Trays* (Alessi, 2004), *Guiyang Tower* (Guiyang China, 2008), Atelier Manferdini. A single pattern of diamond-shaped cuts and folds in the surfaces of a diverse set of objects with different scales and materials yields a variety of effects and behaviors.

The capacity of a relatively simple pattern to embody and adapt to changing material information—information that is arranged to withstand large amounts of geometric deformation—is clearly evident in Reiser + Umemoto's O-14 office tower in Dubai. They add an important property to the diagrid: suppleness. At first glance the exterior bearing wall looks more like a constellation of randomly placed dots than a diagrid. In fact, it is a highly calibrated and topologically generated one comprising four different sizes of filleted diamonds. Despite this simple set of elements, the overall effect is complex.

Less a frame than a flexible web, its spotted sensibility belies its agility in adapting to different operative and environmental requirements. Distortions in what would otherwise be a homogenous pattern are guided by structural analyses, material behavior, the programmatic requirements of the interior, and daylighting studies. While the skin could be optimized for any of the four, an integrative approach results in a combinatorial pattern that performs multiple roles with nuanced optical effects.

Promiscuous Diagrid

If O-14 demonstrates a pattern's ability to incorporate several types of architectural constraints, the work of Atelier Manferdini shows how the same diamond pattern can seamlessly transfer between architecture and other types of design projects. Despite discrepancies in size, function, and material, the two-dimensional pattern—digitally inscribed onto a surface that is subsequently cut, torn, and stretched—produces comparable textures and volumes while functioning differently in each case.

For the Bloom line of mass-customized serving trays, the diamond pattern is water-jet cut from lightweight stainless steel sheets. Here, it not only establishes the visual and tactile qualities of the trays but also guides the physical transformation from flat surface to highly textured and volumetric form by allowing the metal to be folded in place without the need for cold-pressing molds. When the same pattern is used for the Nike AirScale shoe, the function and

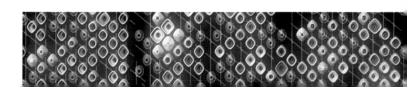

distribution of diamonds is different. The cuts allow for a relatively stiff material to conform to the changing contours of the foot, locally adjusting flexibility and ventilation while guiding the dynamic forces of running and dancing into the sole. When deployed in the Clad Cuts dress design, the laser-cut pattern produces different effects in a less rigid material, provocatively revealing the body as the fabric sags and stretches in response to the highly particular and fluid relationship of pattern, cloth, and movement. For the Guiyang Tower, a larger version of the pattern creates a lacy envelope that performs structurally. As the diamonds vary in density and size, the facade opens and closes to provide a variety of formal, spatial, and lighting effects, while the various layers and orientation of the material are carved to produce unexpectedly delicate results. Because the diagrid is promiscuously deployed across very different scales, materials, and functional criteria—and despite its unique use in each—the four projects are collectively consistent.

Protean Diagrid

If patterns are to function as more than a motif or an expedient design tool, they must be able to produce new environments by linking architecture's internal (that is, formal and spatial) techniques with extradisciplinary knowledge. Their capacity for doing so is granted along three interrelated lines: their redundant qualities, their flexibility, and their combinatory logic.

A pattern's numerous and potentially diverse components and subpatterns typically create rampant redundancies. In redundant systems the removal of any part will not destroy overall performance or legibility. The function of redundancy is to provide continuity of performance; if no single component is critical to the overall operation in a system, then as one part fails or is deformed, other (no longer redundant) components pick up the slack. This is especially true when parts can operate differently over time—a kind of functional and sensory shapeshifting that allows the pattern itself to rapidly fluctuate between various configurations.

Patterns' ability to channel otherwise incompatible informational, organizational, and material inputs further contributes to their vitality. Like neural structures, **patterns make quick and repeatable connections** across highly complex networks of charged gaps and self-similar elements: through graphic and organizational alignments, they catalyze connections between unrelated media; via high resolution multiplicity, they form gradients between binary oppositions; and by way of synaptic adjacencies, they activate relationships between seemingly incongruent material fields. Because of their redundancy, patterns can incorporate multiple and variously structured rhythms, systems, or operations and weave them together to increase responsiveness. Unlike traditionally static and uni-functional patterns, new strains are neither completely predictable nor homogeneous.

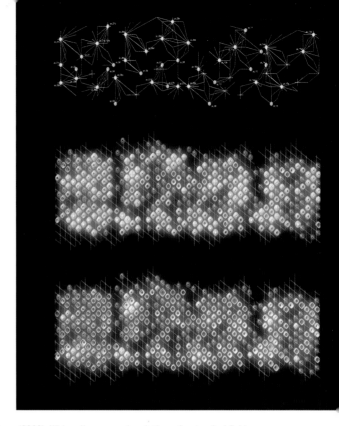

Terminal Life, Responsive Systems Group (2006). Wiring diagram and variations. A networked field of diamond-shaped components can communicate with one another, allowing each component and the system as a whole to react to programmatic and environmental information, and in turn to change its form, lighting, and acoustic properties from one moment to the next.

These capacities and behaviors are evident in *Terminal Life*, a project by the Responsive Systems Group (RSG). The activation of a field of components—provoked by numerous interactions with travelers and the general demands of an airport—produces ambient variations and local irregularities of light, sound, and color. The diamond-shaped cells are affixed to a diagrid substructure and networked with one another so as to operate either independently or in sync, depending on the stimuli they receive from their environments. The system's redundancy (every component is embedded with LED lighting, holosonic speakers, and a kinetic skin even though they are only selectively switched by a network of proximity sensors) and its capacity to locally absorb positive and negative feedback allows for multiscalar variation. In other words the component field can be stable and far from equilibrium at the same time.

The installation—potentially mounted to either a ceiling or wall—is perpetually animated and its appearance is constantly in flux. As the cells extend and retract, open and close, are illuminated and darkened, they generate a seemingly infinite variety of highly patterned visual, acoustic, and atmospheric effects. Binding and enabling the project's behavioral variety is the visual and organizational presence of the diagrid.

The work of Reiser + Umemoto, Atelier Manferdini, and RSG illustrates how advanced breeds of patterns can reestablish the architect as an expert in linking seemingly disparate cultural and epistemological categories. How are optical effects and the compressive strength of concrete related? What does holosonic speaker technology have to do with the behavior of airline passengers? While the juxtapositions seem bizarre, these are the kind of questions that many architects construct and respond to through design projects. At an abstract level, this means accommodating both spatial and temporal demands, integrating material and social behaviors, and combining cultural trends with formal desires. Expanding the types and uses of patterns in architecture is an effective way to develop new models for making such connections.

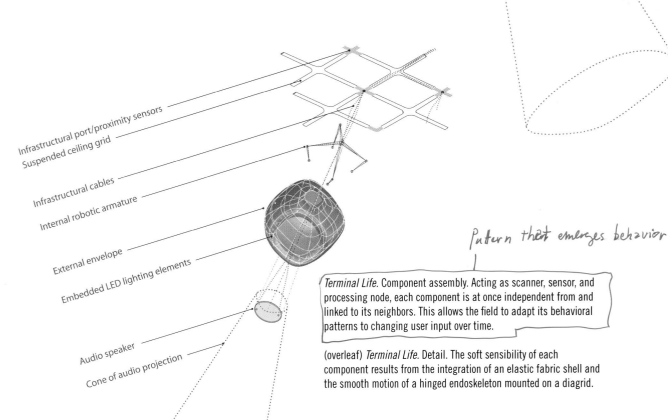

Infrastructural port/proximity sensors

Suspended ceiling grid

Infrastructural cables

Internal robotic armature

External envelope

Embedded LED lighting elements

Audio speaker

Cone of audio projection

Pattern that emerges behavior

Terminal Life. Component assembly. Acting as scanner, sensor, and processing node, each component is at once independent from and linked to its neighbors. This allows the field to adapt its behavioral patterns to changing user input over time.

(overleaf) *Terminal Life.* Detail. The soft sensibility of each component results from the integration of an elastic fabric shell and the smooth motion of a hinged endoskeleton mounted on a diagrid.

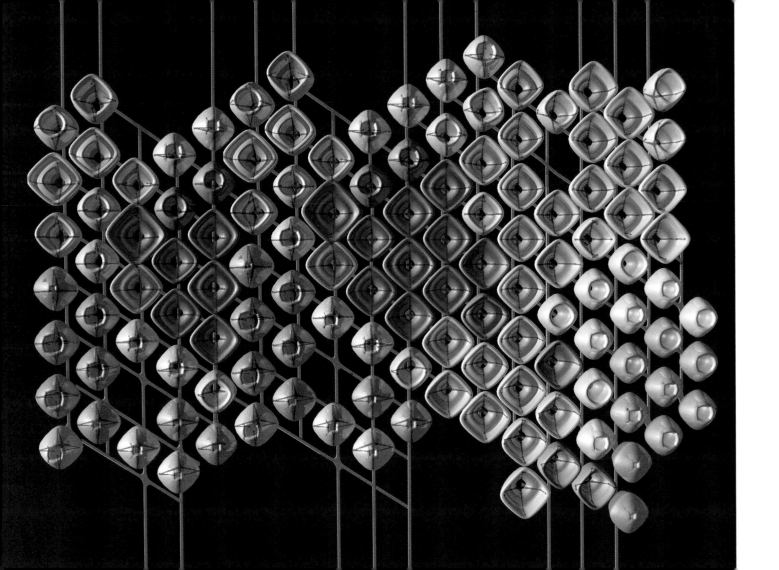

CHAPTER 2 : PRINCIPLES   PRIMITIVES

The Architecture of Pat
Paul Andersen and Da
Anderson and Da
Paul An

There had been no thievery or venality. We had all simply wandered into a situation unthinkingly, trying to protect ourselves from what we saw as a political problem. Now, suddenly, it was like a Rorschach ink blot: others, looking at our actions, pointed out a pattern that we ourselves had not seen.

Richard M. Nixon

As architecture is often perceived to be an accurate and lasting testament to the ethos of an era, its time is measured in decades, never days. Even modernism's alleged attempts to run with technology failed to quicken its pace.[1] Architectural theory has its own durational issues. While almost always presenting itself as of-the-moment, it too dreams of eternity with its perpetual calls to redefine architecture once and for all.

Patterns have conformed to this tempo. From pattern books that catalog ornamental tropes and ever-relevant solutions to be continually copied, to the linguistic and scientific modes of analysis and composition offered up in the 1960s and 1970s by Christopher Alexander and company, to the design codes advocated by the New Urbanists, patterns have been valued for their stable, timeless, and replicable nature. Yet in many design practices (graphic, textile, and industrial, to name a few), patterns are prized for their ephemerality. Predictably, modernists past and present have dismissed this characteristic as frivolous at best, dangerous at worst. Rather than simply exchanging one extreme (slowness) for another (speed), today's malleable patterns slide between these limits. Neither permanent nor whimsical,

these protean versions navigate architecture's competing temporal demands by being at once flexible and multivalent. Their genealogy can be traced to figures outside architecture—namely the chemist Ilya Prigogine and the anthropologist and cyberneticist Gregory Bateson—who, at the same time as Alexander, were developing alternative theories of patterns that have not entered architectural discourse until now. What they claim can lay the groundwork for a new architectural theory of patterns and their potential influence on contemporary practice.

Alexander + Kepes

No one has taken the eternal associations of patterns more seriously than Christopher Alexander. With the publication of *A Pattern Language* in 1977 and *A Timeless Way of Building* in 1979, he and his partners initiated a 30-year monopoly on the topic. During the 1980s the logic developed in those books migrated to computer science and since that time has become increasingly influential in a number of fields. Despite this success, Alexander's stance also reveals the limitations of any theory of patterns that positions them as underlying and unchanging organizations. Specifically, it solidifies the status quo.

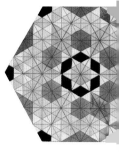

Design for Tiles, Owen Jones (1849). Jones's work and writing documented a wide range of patterning techniques, but also limited their development and deployment to the realm of ornamentation.

159 LIGHT ON TWO SIDES
OF EVERY ROOM**

A Pattern Language, Christopher Alexander (1977). Alexander's bible-like book includes Pattern 159, "Light on Two Sides of Every Room." Alexander's axioms are presented as a do-it-yourself guide, which is the outcome of exhaustive and allegedly incontrovertible empirical evidence.

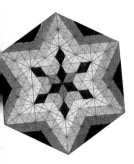

When they have a choice, people will always gravitate to those rooms which have light on two sides, and leave the rooms which are lit only from one side unused and empty.

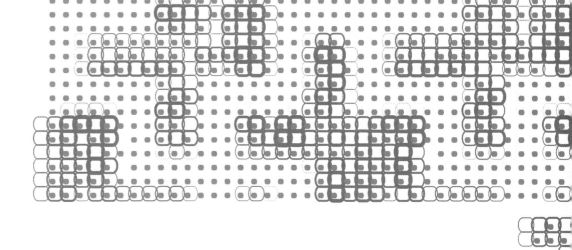

Alexander's position is consistent with most scientific definitions of patterns in that he believes their fundamental order to be capable of explaining the seemingly random parts of the world we occupy. Or, in artificial intelligence pioneer Herbert Simon's words, the task of natural science is "to show that complexity . . . is only a mask for simplicity [and] to find pattern hidden in apparent chaos."[2] According to Alexander's logic, patterns are always present, even when not immediately legible. They can be uncovered with rigorous empirical study, codified, and collected to produce a language that is universally applicable. As Alexander notes, his design process is not based on combining patterns to make new or more complex wholes, but instead is the "unfolding" of an already existing, if not fully understood, code that simply needs to be translated into architecture. Like natural laws, patterns don't change, even if the buildings they create appear to. The function of such patterns is blatantly conservative—they are the means of reducing change and providing comfortable environments for people, environments built on principles that emphasize traditional forms and imagery.

A slightly less conservative understanding of patterns, but one that also directly addressed their ability to traffic between surface appearances and hidden structures, was proposed by the designer and educator Gyorgy Kepes. From the 1940s through the 1960s Kepes edited a series of publications examining the potential integration of science and art. The books were heavily illustrated with photographs of stunning natural patterns, a good number of which are only visible aerially or with the aid of a microscope. The logic of their presentation accentuates affinities with twentieth-century abstract art, proof that aesthetic and scientific practices and forms were linked at a deep level, at the "structure" or "pattern"—terms used often in the accompanying texts.

The combination of arresting images and explanations of the fundamental processes that had produced these patterns (and described in the texts) suggested a more dynamic relationship between morphology and function—a relationship that had obvious methodological implications for architectural design. Kepes recognized that making use of these insights required a more synthetic understanding of the design process—that is, a process that combined scientific and artistic methods of discovery. Patterns were central to this new technique, which would require a "new vision" that would allow one to move beyond "thing seeing" and toward "pattern seeing." This active mode of perception would favor "interactions, not things."[3] According

The New Landscape in Art and Science, edited by Gyorgy Kepes (1966). On the left is a photomicrograph of a cleared leaf and on the right is a photo of a boreo desert. The juxtaposition of similar patterns with radically different scales was offered as proof of recurring, underlying structures that connect various realms of nature.

to Kepes, "although we see it as an entity—unified, distinct from its surroundings—a pattern in nature is a temporary boundary that both separates and connects the past and the future of the processes that trace it. Patterns are the meeting-points of action. Noun and verb must be seen as one: process in patterns, pattern in process."[4]

However, far from creating progressive or extreme solutions, the processes in which Kepes was most interested were ones that maintained formal, social, and geopolitical homeostasis. His attempts "to unify art and science on the common ground of control and communication, with architecture represented as an agent of homeostatic regulation," were one way for postwar culture to maintain what Sigfried Giedion had dubbed "dynamic equilibrium."[5]

Within this cybernetic formulation, stability had to be maintained via the use of negative feedback—a method of response found in natural systems that was increasingly being used to improve the performance of technological devices (namely, weapons systems), as well as to "improve" social

relations between individuals and collectives. Following this line of reasoning, Kepes argued that while "most of the visual patterns of our man-created landscape lack such congruence between process and pattern," the natural patterns made visible by photography "clarify relations of order, continuity and direction in the emergence, growth and disappearance of nature's forms,"[6] and suggested a way of translating these examples of "natural occurring equilibrium" into cultural systems. In each case a self-stabilizing system was dependent on the adjustment of specific components to environmental information.

The extension of negative feedback—where all information that deviates from a desired trajectory is corrected to maintain a predetermined state—into the social arena was aided by a peculiar conception of the human subject itself as a "pattern." For Norbert Wiener, one of the founders of cybernetics, a pattern was a trace of the "homeostatic processes" that allowed organisms to preserve their identity in an otherwise "entropic environment." In other words, a pattern— or "message"—was an arrangement of information

a pa++ern (like one's personality) is relatively malleable

that remained constant, or was capable of reforming, as it interacted with other patterns. More so than any physical consistency, one's identity was marked by the consistent pattern or message that one transmitted to others.

Like any other message, however, it could be miscommunicated. Far from being fixed, a pattern (like one's personality) is relatively malleable, the degree of its flexibility being dependent on its internal properties (its capacity to self-organize) and the entropic intensity of the environment it encounters. The desire to maintain cultural homeostasis and conformity, and thus minimize personal and social disorder, has a variety of social and political pitfalls. For many the definition of individuals as nothing more than coded patterns or messages suggested that they could be easily "reprogrammed" during the exchange of information—an exchange that was increasingly made in the unidirectional and centrally controlled stream of mass media. It also questioned the suitability of architecture as a medium through which messages flow. The capacity to affect a subject and by extension a society—to stabilize and guide them psychologically— through the active management of their environment was a traditionally architectural function that was increasingly being challenged by other media outlets.

Schizo-equilibrium

Despite the dangers posed by a cybernetically monitored society and the loss of architecture's relevance within it, other conclusions can be drawn from Wiener's definition of identity (personal and architectural) as a transmittable pattern and from Kepes's recognition of the pattern as a "temporary boundary." In particular, a more optimistic prognosis is possible when positive, not just negative, feedback is allowed to open up the circuit. In contrast to the elimination of "noise," positive feedback actively adds destabilizing information into exchanges between organisms (or building systems) and their environments, producing states that are far from equilibrium, far from the status quo, and hard to predict. Fashion trends are classic examples—the more people purchase a certain style, the more desirable it is to others who, in turn, buy in, and on and on. Many examples of positive feedback involve this kind of sorting, in which choices are made based on the popularity of earlier choices. As selection progresses, the number of attractive options diminishes and one becomes a clear favorite (often with surprising quickness), producing a new state of equilibrium. When moments of homeostasis are obtained, equilibrium is provisional and multiple—it might be described as schizo-equilibrium instead of dynamic equilibrium.

To produce such a state requires that a pattern remain dependent upon and located within larger systems but not overdetermined by them. Such patterns can be directed from within their own logic and can be more than just the index of other forces. This is especially true of human subjects, cultures, and the artifacts they make, which, unlike natural phenomena, do have the capacity for agency and adaptation in the short term. In other words, patterns need not simply communicate identity; they can actively perform and produce it.

Benard convection cells in a thin layer of silicone oil. This highly articulated pattern is not evidence of stability, as patterns often are in the sciences. It registers a specific moment of consistent molecular behavior within a system that is far from equilibrium.

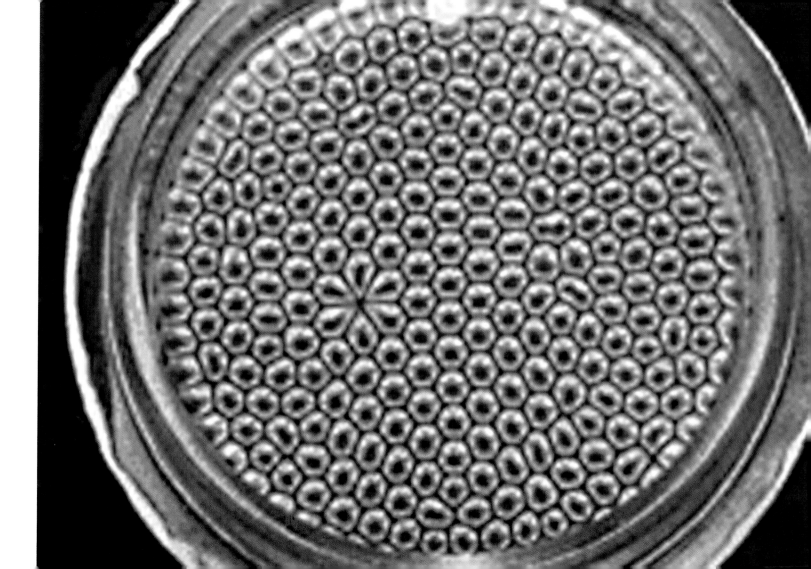

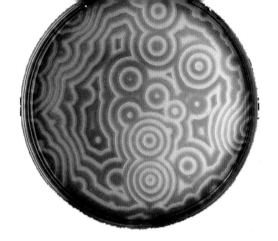

*Oscillating patterns in an excitable medium (Belousov Zhabotinsky reactions).*The volatile and periodically changing patterns in these reactions do not emerge from any known fundamental principles. They are a dynamic material organization that results from mutual interactions between a chemical medium and its environment.

The specific shapes or messages that a pattern "puts on" or morphs into can change but only within the limits set by its initial design. If the original, uninformed pattern is too simple or inflexible, it will be unable to adapt to environmental conditions and will be either isolated or overrun. At the same time, if it too closely resembles its context it risks being overwhelmed or disappearing into its milieu—a condition that is equally true for individuals as well as for buildings, building systems, and urban landscapes.

As Ilya Prigogine's research proved, similarly active patterns are evident in chemical processes. Before his discoveries, most physicists, mathematicians, chemists, and biologists viewed behavioral and morphogenetic patterns as registrations of unchanging structural principles. He proposed a relationship between form and behavior that is much more capricious, challenging the predominantly indexical association of patterns and scientific laws.

In 1977, the same year in which Alexander published *A Pattern Language*, Prigogine won the Nobel Prize in Chemistry for his work in dissipative structures. Unlike Alexander's interest in stability, Prigogine's research focused on the behavior of systems far from equilibrium, ones that exchange energy with the environments around them.[7]

A thin layer of boiling liquid is an example: energy in the form of heat is introduced from below and lost to cooler air above. While most far from equilibrium systems are characterized by chaotic motion and unpredictable concoctions of matter, occasionally they organize in patterns. Dissipative structures are one such patterned organization—for instance, Benard convection cells that momentarily appear as hexagonally shaped bubbles on the bottom of the container of boiling liquid. Heat from the burner causes some molecules to gain energy and rise until they lose that energy to the cooler air above and begin to sink again. At first, they exhibit Brownian motion, a more or less random movement, but once the temperature reaches a certain threshold a pattern of convection cells forms. As the temperature increases further, cells disappear and the fluid returns to a state of chaotic turbulence. Prigogine argued that these complex patterns (which also include the Belousov-Zhabotinsky reaction and storms such as cyclones) form when the system develops an asymmetrical relationship with its surroundings and its uniform "thermodynamic branch" becomes unstable. In these cases, patterns are volatile and transitory.

Like the patterns documented by Kepes, the behavior described by Prigogine is produced through exchanges between an open system (or, in the case of Kepes, an

organism) and its environment. But contrary to Kepes's and Alexander's use of patterns as mechanisms for maintaining identity in an entropic, chaotic world—supported by the isolationism of thermodynamics—Prigogine's patterns are coincidental with high degrees of flux; they only appear under circumstances of dynamic instability. Feedback between a system's agents, whether direct or through their local environments, sets off rapid, cascading changes to a dissipative structure.

Prigogine's theories have been hotly contested, particularly the relationship between patterns and the laws that govern them. Philip W. Anderson, another Nobelist, places dissipative structures in the realm of transitory effects rather than stable patterns, and, in doing so, sustains a conception of the pattern as a permanent and essential condition. Despite the visually repetitive nature of dissipative structures, Anderson is reluctant to call them patterns because he believes them to be uniquely formed in each case rather than governed by broad fundamental principles. Anderson's critique underscores a similarly structural role for patterns in the work of Prigogine, who uses them to extrapolate a new dynamics for unstable systems from the thermodynamic laws that apply in equilibrium. He argues that there are no such fundamentals to be found in Prigogine's patterns; rather, they

are only complex physical behaviors read against a backdrop of chaotic noise. Yet his dismissal contains a new definition of patterns, when he acknowledges "their ability to lead to the emergent property of spatial variation from a homogeneous background."[8] He concedes an essential shift in the perceived capacity of patterns—no longer the harbingers of dynamic equilibrium, they are liberated to catalyze qualitative diversity.

For architecture, the ways in which this debate reformulates the notion of a pattern are more important than who is correct. From Prigogine we get an interpretation of the pattern as a condition of instability embedded in an entropic and unpredictable environment, rather than juxtaposed to it. In other words, a pattern is an organization that a system expands into rather than an underlying structure to which it can be reduced. Meanwhile, Anderson's critique affirms that since no universal laws govern these types of patterns, each is provisional and local.

This suggests new possibilities for patterns in design: first, to incorporate any number of distinct forms within a continuum of time or space; second, to be multiple and changing in any one project; third, to be as much or more the outward appearance of a project as its deep structure; and fourth, to react mutually with their physical and social environments.

" Gregory Bateson suggested a similarly flexible view of patterns in his 1979 book, *Mind and Nature: A Necessary Unity,* in which he identified "the pattern that connects" as providing an epistemological link between the natural and the cultural. At first glance, this definition appears analogous to Christopher Alexander's totalizing ideology. Similarly, it echoes Gyorgy Kepes's argument that an aesthetic sensibility can better join things than segregate them. While related to these other thinkers, Bateson's understanding and use of pattern contains important differences—differences that have distinct advantages for architecture.

For Bateson, patterns operate according to an aesthetic logic—one that is based on "recognition and empathy" rather than rationality.[9] But while he describes the general continuity between mind and nature as a "metapattern," he proposes that patterns are neither teleological nor eternal but recursive. Thus, his definition of patterns is much more fluid than Alexander's or Kepes's: "We have been trained to think of patterns, with the exception of those of music, as fixed affairs. It is easier and lazier that way but, of course, all nonsense. In truth, the right way to begin to think about the pattern which connects is to think of it as primarily (whatever that means) a dance of interacting parts and only secondarily pegged down by various sorts of physical limits and by those limits which organisms characteristically impose."[10]

While this echoes Kepes's interpretation—with its emphasis on the temporal quality of "the pattern that connects" and an organism's role in its genesis—it also recognizes that not only are the physical manifestations produced by underlying rules subject to change, but the metapatterns are themselves also vulnerable to loss and differentiation from external forces. In other words, they are susceptible to positive as well as negative feedback.

Bateson's dance metaphor is a particularly robust and illustrative one. There are at least three intertwining yet distinct patterns in any dance: the choreography, the music, and the bodies of the performers. Like all patterns, all three can be literally and accurately described in terms of the relationship between identical or self-similar parts. However, what remains somewhat outside the realm of patterns, but is nevertheless generated from the combination of them, is the performance of the dance itself. In cybernetic terms, the performance (itself a mixture of specific temporal and physical acts) is outside the system—it is "noise." Every instantiation of a choreographed dance is part of a iterative and stochastic system; one that is at once predictable (the noted steps) and random (the interpretation by the dancers). For Bateson, randomness and noise are not nuisances to be eliminated but a necessity to be cultivated. He notes that

"all that is not information, not redundancy, not form, and not restraints—is noise, the only possible source of new patterns."[11]

Redundancy + Newness

Bateson argues that a pattern's paradoxical proclivity for creating newness out of consistency is a function of redundancy, or the predictability of particular events in the context of a larger collective of events.[12] The sequential repetition of similar parts within a pattern allows one to forecast the next iteration, and once the rules of combination between the parts are established (in music, on a facade, in a text, or on a piece of fabric) any deviation will stand out (and is coded positively as information or negatively as a mistake). This is true even within highly intricate patterns, where idiosyncrasies may be more difficult to identify.

Bateson's argument is self-consciously framed within the cybernetic discourse on communication,

organization, thought, learning, and evolution. Unlike the laws that govern energy and mass, when the science of organization is applied to social relationships involving communication between people, there are no "natural" rules to prevent noise—any deviation from what's expected.[13] For Bateson, such deviations are not a problem to be eradicated but are necessary for learning to occur. The emergence of "foreign" parts within seemingly fixed patterns is evidence of the pattern's embedded nature and propels the evolution of stochastic processes. This insight enabled him to recognize the differences and relationships between epigenetic growth and processes of evolution and learning.[14]

Morphological development in epigenetic processes is an unfolding of an already complete whole, where parts are developed through a sequence of divisions or differentiations. This is precisely the analogy Alexander uses to describe his "Timeless Way,"[15] a method in which the architect nurses an embryo-building to maturity. The designer protects the embryo from external forces through the elimination of random or superficial components. Alexander's patterns only contain information that is always present in a given spatial type. In cybernetic terms, his process is one in which negative feedback

is aggressively administered to identify and eliminate noise—any element within an architectural pattern that is not essential—to maintain the pattern's homeostatic and therefore idealized status. In contrast, evolution and learning are acts of accretion, of making a complex whole from independent but related parts. Evolutionary design requires the coordination of programmatic information from internal and external sources.

While the unfolding of embryology deals with reason and replication, evolution is the domain of creativity, art, learning—practices that produce change. A combination of predictability and randomness generates new varieties of patterns without devolving into a chaotic state. In both language-based and biological systems, patterns are a form of repetition in which iterative components allow one to make educated guesses about what's not yet present. In Bateson's words, "To guess, in essence, is to face a cut or slash in the sequence of items and to predict across that slash what items might be on the other side. The slash may be spatial or temporal (or both) and the guessing may be either predictive or retrospective. A pattern, in fact, is definable as an aggregate of events or objects which will permit such guesses when the entire aggregate is not available for inspection."[16]

Because of their predictability, patterns prepare one to receive random input, helping to select what will be reintegrated as new information; information that can thrive in an unfamiliar context by adapting to, or modifying, the patterns that preceded it. Thus, far from maintaining homogeneity or encouraging pandemonium, patterns establish favorable conditions for creativity and learning to occur. Since their inherent repetition allows parts to be immediately recognized, the addition of new information can be registered against this known background, in turn producing new information and a new pattern. Legible deformations of a once-regular pattern are thus never simply an index of the forces acting on it. Because the original state is still present and somewhat recognizable, the base array's identity remains separate yet linked to these forces. Located on a continuum between constant and random, the resultant pattern is both flexible and specific.

Plurality

Informed speculation is particularly important in such design problems, where there is more than one "correct" answer. This is especially true for architects, whose task is, in part, to imagine new alternatives to what already exists. Bateson makes explicit the relationship between what is and what could be when he argues, "With almost no exceptions, the behaviors called art or their products (also called art) have two characteristics: they require or exhibit skill, and they contain redundancy or pattern. But those two characteristics are not separate: the skill is first in maintaining and then in modulating the redundancies."[17]

There are two levels of redundancy: the first is a perfect replication of a form, figure, or graphic, and the second is a differentiated version of the first. Together they account for the "linkage in aesthetics between skill and pattern" and register a development away from the original. The pure repetition of the first-level redundancy serves as a baseline against which the variation of the second-level redundancy can be read. This process produces "multileveled knowledge": the proficiency required for the first level enables the innovation of the second. In such a scenario,

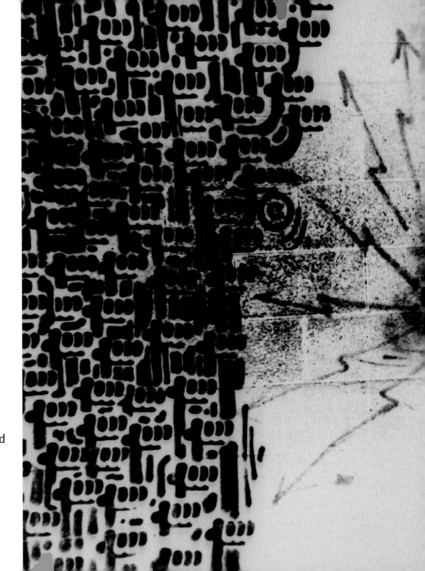

==design becomes the skillful manipulation of excess and repetition==—patterns—such that they produce novel, if slightly familiar, outcomes. Ever stochastic, patterns enable the new to emerge out of the same, repeating the difference in them, not only the same we want to see.

Recap

For Alexander patterns are the stable laws (the unfolding of epigenetic logic) that make sense of chaos; for Kepes they are agents of homeostasis; and for Bateson they are relatively stable but flexible original materials, a design primitive, on which outside agents act. ==They target what could be designed rather than what should be.==

In both cultural and natural systems, patterns have the ability to adapt their internal, autonomous logics to external, heterogeneous forces without losing either their aesthetic or organizational identity. The combination of these typically independent systems does not produce overly smooth solutions that neutralize the specific traits of any one of them. Instead, it results in highly calibrated, particular, yet easily recognizable ad-mixtures; aggregations where both the gestalt of a primitive pattern and the individual events or distortions within it are alternatively highlighted or hidden according to the specific demands—formal and functional—that satisfies at any one moment.

The redundancies present in patterns—emphasized by Bateson and found in today's "thick" and protean architectural patterns—are neither excessive nor efficient; they neither optimize nor essentialize any one aspect of a design; instead redundancies enable a pattern and the elements within it to act as a diagram that anticipates multiple informational and energy flows. A newly theorized understanding of patterns—focusing on the flexible and multifunctional capabilities made possible by their redundant characteristics—encourages patterns' surplus repetition to function as a force for maximizing technical, sensory, and aesthetic capacities.

CHAPTER 3 : VARIATION + VARIETY

Adaptability is not imitation. It means power of resistance and assimilation.

Mahatma Gandhi

The Architecture of
Paul Andersen and
Paul Andersen at

The recent re-emergence of patterns in contemporary architecture can partly be understood as a reassessment of the isolationist tendencies present in both modern and post-modern theories of architecture. Many of those theories denied the generalist potential of architecture. In typically paradoxical fashion, a new understanding of architectural patterns maintains the emphasis on performance and aesthetic coherence found in modernism, while incorporating the indexicality, hybridity, and ambiguity of post-modernism.

In modernism superfluous or multi-functional components were discouraged; formal conformity was encouraged; and excesses of any kind were typically eliminated from the design equation. While post-modernism (in both its historicist and deconstructivist iterations) accepted hybrid solutions and elements, they were manifested in a logic as similarly divided as the modernist one it sought to replace. While the former failed to create well-oiled architectural and urban machines and instead produced a series of disconnected objects, functional

zones, and social classes, the latter could do no better than expose this segregationist attitude, before eventually reproducing it. The result of these divisive definitions was that architectural expertise and form were both culturally isolated and internally fragmented. In other words, the projects of self-rationalizing and of re-complexification drained architecture of its most valuable asset: its ability to function across disciplinary boundaries and connect otherwise disconnected topics and phenomena.

The historical arc of this paradigm shift moves from a modernist call for progress, through a post-modern call for meaning, to the more recent interest in variation, and now to the prospect of increased variety.[18] Until today, the shift had mirrored a similar trajectory in evolutionary biology, where the concept of a species evolving toward an ever-more-advanced state has been replaced by the value of nonhierarchical variation between and among species.[19] Patterns are particularly useful devices for converting biological processes of adaptation and variation into design techniques. As graphics and as diagrams, they have persistent visual identities and organizational predilections, but they also have the flexibility to respond to any number of situational factors. The ways in which they can be modified—digitally and materially—have mushroomed in recent years, giving them a pervasive presence in different stylistic camps. A wide range of contemporary projects deploy patterns in the pursuit of difference within a prescribed set of rules: dynamism tempered with equilibrium. Variation is, by definition, constrained. It internalizes difference. Endless variations on a single pattern (say, the grid) are possible, transformation being a function of how it incorporates external influences, or noise. But when one pattern merges with another, closed and open systems of difference can coexist. This indiscriminate blend is not endemic to biology (the mixing of species is technically impossible, socially disdainful, and ethically intolerable for most) nor to the vast majority of architectural projects.

To create patterns that adeptly channel intensive variation and also provide extensive variety, we must look beyond biological processes to more synthetic examples of pattern making, namely those found in art. When patterns are created by designers, the concept of genres takes over that of species, opening up the possibility of cross-categorical exchange, of short circuiting the very boundaries that define variation. With the potential to incorporate the double difference of variation and variety, patterns can broker architectural innovation by elevating an aesthetic logic of connection, of "evolution and learning."[20] We find in them combinations of intensity and promiscuity that point the way toward new forms of identity and intelligence in architecture in particular and in culture in general.

From Basic to Basal

The design primitive has been a common starting point for architectural variation in recent years. Although the term "primitive" has a checkered history (not dissimilar to patterns)—namely for its use as a synonym for ethnic or cultural inferiority—certain definitions in architectural discourse are relevant to pattern-based design practices. Architectural primitives include original and ideal geometric forms (for example, spheres and cubes); a codified set of relationships between parts; idealized projects and practices; and organizational diagrams. Historical examples—which include the ancient orders, Platonic solids, typologies, styles, grids, and the nine-square—share the property of malleability; they are embedded with various lines of development that can be enacted via design decisions that actively inform them (more information amounts to a more specific variant of the primitive).

"Primitive" invokes a number of associations and functions, but perhaps the most useful ones for architecture today come from mathematics and evolutionary biology. In mathematics a primitive is something basic or prime; primitive polynomials are irreducible ones; the primitive element theorem in field theory characterizes finite field extensions that are simple; and perhaps most important for architects, primitive geometries are elemental figures and forms from which more complex geometries can be constructed. For example, any polygon, no matter how irregular or elaborate, is an accumulation of triangles and, conversely, triangles are the primitive geometry of every polygon.

Such primitives show up in calculus-based software platforms, such as Maya, but are not necessarily treated as basic elements. In Greg Lynn's Embryologic Houses, for example, the primitive—a spheroid—functions less as a building block than as an adaptive organism. Instead of amassing spheres to generate a complex envelope, a single spheroid is flooded with programmatic, topographic, and climatic information that distorts its original and ideal form. While the project's primitive is a basic form, as in mathematics, the techniques used to make its specific variations open the door to an architecture that is more basal.

If basic forms are irreducible elements that a designer aggregates to generate complex assemblies, basal forms are characterized as being in an early stage of development relative to similar forms. In cladistics, the most prominent of several forms of phylogenetics (the study of how different organisms are related in terms of their evolution), primitive organisms are considered basal, meaning that they diverged from the evolutionary line earlier than comparative coexisting groups. For example, the orangutan is the most basal of the great apes. In this view, any particular form is considered to be a singular instance within a larger group, with no prejudice for, or necessary reference to, an ideal origin or outcome. Simple variations are not inferior, but are instead believed to have quickly adapted to the demands placed on them and have required no further evolution to respond to changes in those demands—in fact, subgroups that stabilize in more simple states are often very well suited to a particular set of commonly occurring circumstances.

With basal forms, because the variation from simple to complex is not hierarchical, the cumulative differences between group members are more valuable than progress toward a state of maximized simplicity or

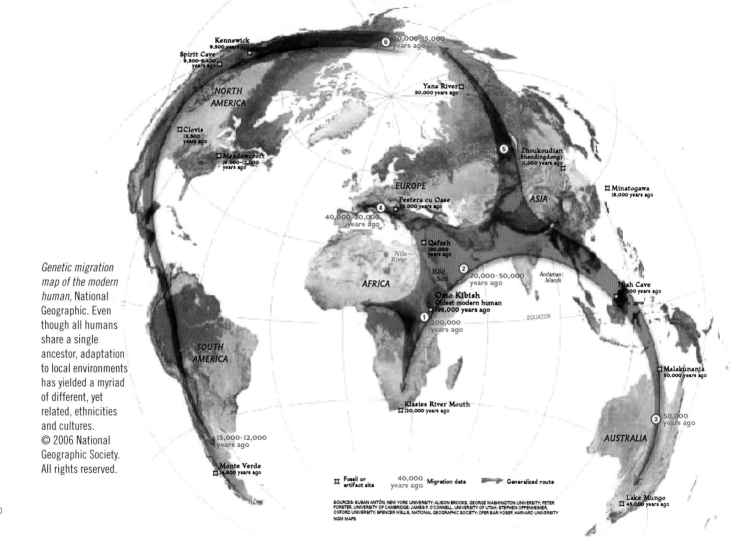

Kennewick
9,500 years ago

Spirit Cave
9,500-9,400
years ago

20,000-15,000
years ago ⑥

Yana River ☐
30,000 years ago

NORTH
AMERICA

☐ Clovis
13,500
years ago

☐ Meadowcroft
19,000-12,000
years ago

40,000
years ago ⑤

Zhoukoudian
(Shandingdong)
11,000 years ago ☐

☐ Minatogawa
18,000 years ago

EUROPE

Pestera cu Oase
☐ 35,000 years ago

ASIA

④

40,000-30,000
years ago

☐ Qafzeh
100,000
years ago

Nile
River

Andaman
Islands

*Genetic migration
map of the modern
human,* National
Geographic. Even
though all humans
share a single
ancestor, adaptation
to local environments
has yielded a myriad
of different, yet
related, ethnicities
and cultures.
© 2006 National
Geographic Society.
All rights reserved.

Red
Sea

②

70,000-50,000
years ago

Niah Cave
years ago ☐

AFRICA

Omo Kibish
Oldest modern human
195,000 years ago

①

200,000
years ago

EQUATOR

SOUTH
AMERICA

☐ Malakunanja
50,000 years ago

Klasies River Mouth
☐ 120,000 years ago

③

50,000
years ago

15,000-12,000
years ago

AUSTRALIA

Monte Verde
14,800 years ago

☐ Fossil or
artifact site

40,000
years ago

Migration date

Generalized route

Lake Mungo
☐ 45,000 years ago

SOURCES: SUSAN ANTÓN, NEW YORK UNIVERSITY; ALISON BROOKS, GEORGE WASHINGTON UNIVERSITY; PETER
FORSTER, UNIVERSITY OF CAMBRIDGE; JAMES F. O'CONNELL, UNIVERSITY OF UTAH; STEPHEN OPPENHEIMER,
OXFORD UNIVERSITY; SPENCER WELLS, NATIONAL GEOGRAPHIC SOCIETY; OFER BAR-YOSEF, HARVARD UNIVERSITY
NGM MAPS

could these relate to how architectural variety & diversification becomes more personalized?

complexity. The consequences of basal thinking for design are that: one, initial conditions are a relative stage of development rather than a quality of irreducibility; and two, development of variations is inherently multilinear. **The evolution of forms is more a process of diversification than improvement**—a way for species to adjust to and even expand their habitats by developing new varieties, rather than by perfecting a universal one.

In evolutionary biology, adaptation is the prime producer of basal variation. As a basal organism proliferates, it encounters and adjusts to different environmental constraints that diversify its overall population. For people, expanding our habitat has resulted in the invention of a variety of cultures that respond to technological and geographical contingencies. Humans have proven to be adept at adapting ourselves to new environments—no matter how isolated or remote—while remaining a coherent species.

Evidence of this exists even at the genetic level. The human genome is 99.9 percent identical throughout the world, so what's left is the DNA responsible for our individual traits—eye color, predispositions for certain diseases, and overall ethnicity,

for example. And while typically reshuffled in the process of reproduction, some markers of those traits, known as mitochondrial DNA, or mtDNA, are passed down intact. In the mid-1980s the late Allan Wilson used mtDNA to trace humanity's ancestral history on the scale of tens of thousands of years, eventually back to Africa. The logic is as follows: women of African descent show twice as much diversity in their mtDNA as their non-African counterparts, and since the telltale mutations occur at a steady rate, modern humans must have lived in Africa twice as long as anywhere else. In fact, scientists now calculate that all living humans are related to a single woman who lived roughly 150,000 years ago in Africa, a Mitochondrial Eve. Only a handful of people, carrying a few of the markers, walked out of Africa and, during the past 70,000 years, seeded other lands (a migration that has been mapped using fossil evidence). In other words, the genetic makeup of the world is a subset of what's in Africa.[21] Boccioni's 1911 statement, "We are the primitives of a new culture," has become scientific fact with unexpected literalness, the human genome being one of the world's most sophisticated base-primitives.

Designing Adaptation

If in evolutionary biology adaptation is typically described as a necessary and unconscious response to a change in an organism's environment, in design this process is actively directed by a designer, who mediates conflicting conditions through invention. Though administered, it is also contingent.

For Herbert Simon, founding father of artificial intelligence, the control of adaptive processes is the way to a "science of design": a speculative effort at establishing not what things are, but what they might be.[22] He identifies the agents of adaptive processes—inner and outer environments, a system objective, and the means of achieving it—and relationships between them as exemplified by various animals, economic models, and machines. His approach situates the designer as a choreographer of relatively simple and repetitive interactions between generally variable and codependent components, which as a system yield multiple and diverse adaptations. The agent that varies least in Simon's description is

the inner environment and, as a result, heterogeneity is a function of contingency in outer environments and the mechanisms of adaptation used in response.

The implements and techniques of adaptation vary, but in architecture there are two discernible operations: **adaptive translation and adaptive specification**. Both approaches disseminate patterns, but in different ways. The first, a kind of duplication, is closest to the biological definition of adaptation and involves the displacement and subsequent reconfiguration of a technique, tool, or form. It entails identifying untapped potential in something designed for and working in one context, transposing it to another arena, and altering the copy to fit its new contingencies. In the last decade, designers have imported software programs, fabrication technologies, and materials from other fields into architectural design. Or, in a case of evolutionary recircuiting, the Bjarke Ingels Group (BIG) moves entire building designs from one project/site/program to another. In this version of adaptive translation, functional migration is high. The same base version works equally well at different scales and with different programs of use.

Symmetrical + Mechanical Pa++erns

Adaptive specification, the second type, begins with standardized, idealized, or generic devices—which may be forms, patterns, or models whose intended purpose is initially far less legible. It involves the simultaneous generation of similar entities with a common source but differing contingencies. Frank Lloyd Wright often used the same methods of subdivision for street patterns, facades, glazing, furniture, and ornament, for example. In this version, typological migration is high. Multiple versions are generated as a base model is reproduced across wildly divergent scalar indices and modes of actualization.[23]

In both examples a productive misalignment is present—in the former between architectural form, location, and function, and in the latter between form and scale. The function of design is not to reconcile or eradicate this gap, rather, it is mobilized to exploit and exaggerate it. Design is not understood as a process of conforming to a norm, but of adapting these norms to a new context; in turn producing new basal states.

like evolution of what I call architectural institutions:
↳ deconstuctivist parallel here?

The human race diversified biologically as it settled in different regions of the globe and populations' cultural practices developed concomitant variation in parallel. The geographically and historically charged differences in the ways people perform tasks common to all humanity can be broadly defined as culture.[24] As with similarities in DNA, cultures—despite obvious differences—share a great deal with one another; each needing to develop a way of producing its food, clothing, shelter, language, religion, political structures, social networks, and artistic practices. What distinguishes one from another is less what issues they deal with than how they deal with them. Or, as the art critic Dave Hickey puts it, style is cultural content.[25] Here too, the concept of basal is a useful substitute for "primitive." Rather than viewing cultures as more or less advanced, an understanding of them as relatively basal (each adapted to its particular context) recognizes the value of all cultures, and cultural variation above all else.

The question of how one does what one does is relevant for all modes of production, from industrial to artistic. The relationship between patterns and production, with its capacity for adaptation and variation, is well established, especially in the decorative arts. The numerous examples of symmetrical patterns found in everyday activities and objects—across geographically and temporally dispersed cultures—have been of particular interest to anthropologists and art historians. To many, their ubiquity across eras and regions proves that there is a common, deep structure that links cultures to one another.[26] And the continual presence of certain motifs and practices, particularly symmetrical ones, serves as evidence of historical continuity and stability. In each case, similarity and homeostasis are privileged over difference and change.

In studying the weaving practices of Peru's Chincero women, anthropologists Christine and Edward Franquemont observed a culture whose lives are permeated by symmetry, in their thinking and action as well as in their arts. With a small repertoire of operations—doubling, division, rotation, translation, reflection, among others—they have generated a seemingly endless repertoire of motifs. The Franquemonts argue that the same set of operations also defines the relationship between genders, between the young and old,

and between the living and the dead. For example, the way a master weaver and a young apprentice sit on the ground, the location of their hands, and the movement of wool as it goes back and forth between them all exhibit the same principles of symmetry found in the motifs themselves. These principles also structure the general division of labor between men and women, and determine the time in a women's life when she will (in adolescence and post-child-rearing age) and when she won't (child-rearing age, when her primary job is agricultural in nature) be actively involved in weaving. And, while symmetry generates incredible variation from one textile to the next, it also guarantees cultural continuity within and across generations. Such consistency among mental, material, and spiritual activities, it is argued, has allowed the culture to thrive despite several periods of colonization. [27]

The multifunctional symmetry that structures the habitus of the Chinchero reveals an extraordinarily high degree of adaptive translation. A single, symmetrical pattern is often exchanged between artifacts and social rules—such as when the same relationships govern the geometry of a motif that appears on a textile, the methods used to produce that

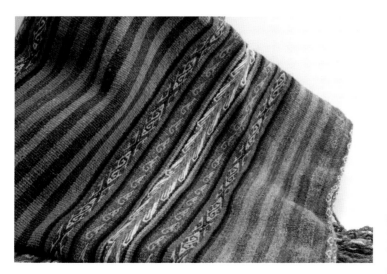

Chincero blanket. A limited set of rules, techniques, and meanings govern the unique internal composition of each weaving. Despite the endurance of these limitations across generations, a great amount of variety is possible from one weaving to the next.

Chincero weavers at the loom. The symmetry of each weaver's location, orientation, and movements is coordinated with symmetries in the textiles themselves.

motif, and the relationship between the master and apprentice who work together to create it. The sum of the Chinchero's cultural weaving practices is also highly basal. Within their patterns, perpetually expanding variation takes precedence over progress from or toward any ideal. While limited to a fixed set of rules, the robustness and depth of their use produces a complex aesthetic well adapted to the Chinchero's geographical context and political history.

As illustrated by the Chinchero, symmetry and symmetrical patterns can produce intricate and sophisticated objects and behaviors; ones geared toward collective variation, rather than an ideal state. They also reveal, however, the limits of such internalized systems. Despite the visual and intellectual rigor, richness, and intricacy of the patterns illustrated by the Franquemonts, they consolidate possibilities rather than expand them. They are not proliferated to form new genres and always resemble the codes from which they came. They are reproductive, but not evolutionary.

Contaminated Pa++erns

From the Vitruvian orders, to Durand's Precis, to Christopher Alexander's Pattern Language, the history of architecture is filled with attempts to systematize architectural design by adopting a set of geometric, symmetric, or cybernetic rules. In all cases the goal is to create a code that governs all areas of architectural production, distribution, and consumption.

In attempting to harness the power of the most advanced mechanical and informational techniques, modernism takes this desire one step further, looking again for one way of thinking and making that could account for all aspects of architectural thought and creation. No matter what the cultural context, there is relatively little difference in how things are to be done; there is only one style. The swift incorporation of serial modes of production into architecture suggests that architects did not adapt them, but uncritically adopted them. This is true even of the seemingly pluralistic nature of "mass customization," which has as its goal an infinite number of "markets of one." For, even when everything is made

CELL

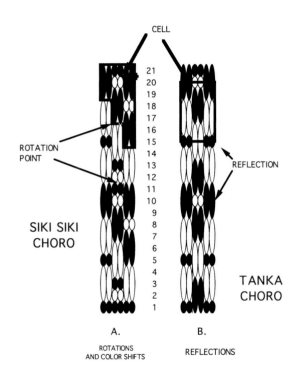

SIKI SIKI
CHORO

ROTATION
POINT

21
20
19
18
17
16
15
14
13
12
11
10
9
8
7
6
5
4
3
2
1

REFLECTION

TANKA
CHORO

A.

ROTATIONS
AND COLOR SHIFTS

B.

REFLECTIONS

Chincero weaving diagrams. Weaving techniques
produce polyscalar symmetry in Chincero textiles.

"just for you," everything is made the same way, using the same digital techniques. There is not a specific code that governs everything, but everything is governed by codes.

As early as the 1950s, the aesthetic and ideological pros and cons of the grid—the most common modernist pattern—had been recognized.[28] More recently, it has been argued that modern painting's combined emphasis on the grid and vision was analogous to past eras' use of symmetry—that is, it allowed for wildly varying sensibilities, from Mondrian to Martin.[29] Such differences could only be made within a bounded set of innovations. Despite his own commitment to examining the potential for difference found in symmetrical operations, it was the polymath Arthur Loeb who identified their aesthetic and mathematical limits. Even as he acknowledged that the seven one-dimensional and seventeen two-dimensional patterns identified by crystallography strictly restricted the formal possibilities of symmetry, he noticed that by combining these 24 base patterns with one another, it is possible to generate a literally infinite number of new ones (topologically speaking).

Variety can be achieved by producing impure and complex blends.[30] For architecture, this might mean that instead of using a structural grid as the module from which all other dimensional and aesthetic decisions are derived, one would need to generate and integrate a variety of patterns from a variety of sources into a more diverse whole. Combining multiple patterns, each of which can include different components, opens up a project's aesthetic identity and organizational logic—it is possible to merge qualities of both, and by doing so, to have the rigor of variation and the promiscuity of variety.

This heterogeneity is antithetical to the essentialist and atomist logic of mechanical production. Rather, such creative leaps are closer to the processes and logic of art. In contrast to modernism's mechanistic and codified modes of production, the shapeshifting capabilities of today's patterns have the potential to break from the vast but ultimately limited scope of variation. They are multifarious, meteoric, elastic, impermanent, sensually immediate, diverse, and quantifiable; qualities that make them effective purveyors of variation and variety. The synthesis of these two kinds of difference—the internal intricacy of variation and the open impurity of variety—can be found in the sensory immediacy and aesthetic diversity of much pattern-based art; art that is produced via recursive and stochastic processes and that

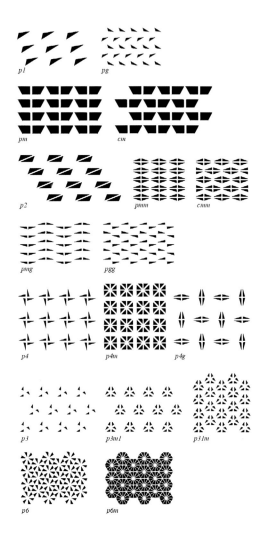

p1　　　pg

pm　　　cm

p2　　　pmm　　cmm

pmg　　　pgg

p4　　　p4m　　p4g

p3　　　p3m1　　p31m

p6　　　p6m

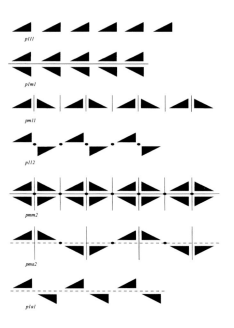

p111

p1m1

pm11

p112

pmm2

pma2

p1a1

Seven types of one-dimensional planar symmetry and seventeen types of two-dimensional planar symmetry. These base patterns are derived from crystallography. All other symmetrical motifs are either combinations or hybrids of these operations.

incorporates external and random inputs.[31] Typical of all evolutionary processes that produce change, the current bio-mathematical paradigm provides architects ever more sophisticated methods of breeding internal variation. One must look to art to find their confluence with variety.

Pa++erns in Op Art

At the same time that arguments for generating a homeostatic synthesis between art and science were being made, another movement was generating a unique mixture of patterns, intuition, technology, symmetry, and pop culture: Op Art.[32] For some, Op was just another example of art illustrating scientific ideas (specifically in optics and perception). For others, both its power and its danger lie in the sometimes pleasurable, sometimes unnerving effects that it generated. Either way, it was quickly and successfully dismissed by the art establishment as a superficial, misplaced, and dangerous gimmick. By ignoring the categorical disparity between two

areas of knowledge, reason and sensation, it allegedly denied art's ability to act as a foil, if not an antidote, to the rampant technological utopianism of the time. Further, the work's quick appropriation by the culture industry—Op's eye-bending graphics appeared on Fifth Avenue dresses and head shop posters in Greenwich Village—served to reinforce the criticism that they were both superficial and scientifically suspect.[33]

In contrast with abstract expressionism, which at its extreme was a direct articulation of an individual's psyche, Op was more populist, accessible, and cooler. Yet, like much abstract expressionism, it was automated; only the reflexive action took place not in the artist's subconscious during production, but in the eye of the viewer. Responses ranged from the pleasure of perceived movement or color changes generated by static forms, to the uncontrolled and more haptic responses of restlessness, dizziness, and nausea.

For some, this represented one of the best examples of **a particular definition of aesthetics: knowledge of the world acquired via sensory experience;** providing insight without conscious or language-based thought. It was cognitive, in an intuitive way.[34]

In January 1965, the Museum of Modern Art launched The Responsive Eye exhibition, a landmark event that, like Kepes's books, used patterned images to solidify the ties between art and science. It is the museum's most visited show to date and its purpose, in the view of curator William Seitz, was to call for the integration of art and science via perception. Equally appalled by its adoption in pop culture and dismayed by its association with scientific methods, the show's reluctant poster-child, Bridget Riley, immediately and consistently distanced herself from these readings. Eschewing all but the most rudimentary mathematical operations, she defined her highly patterned paintings in purely disciplinary terms, her themes and tropes coming out of her own rigorous study of painting, and her method for generating and evaluating effects a ruthlessly empirical one of trial and error.[35] Not dependent on rules of science or mathematics, Riley worked in the realm of haptic vision, emphasizing direct and visceral relationships between subject and objects. If for no other reason, the consistency with which Riley produced such effects distinguishes her work from that of other Op artists.

For Riley, patterns are the source and billboard of style. Her skill in manipulating them is what makes her work recognizable, transgressive, and above all, exotic. As Dave Hickey describes them, "the comfort of the familiar always bore with it the frisson of the exotic, and the effect of this conflation, ideally was persuasive excitement—visual pleasure. As Baudelaire says, 'the beautiful is always strange,' by which he means, of course, that it's always strangely familiar."[36]

At first glance, Riley's paintings appear to be made up of relatively simple, repetitive structures. A list of the motifs used in her work of the early to mid-1960s—stripes, grids, dots, zigzags, waves—reads like the table of contents of a fabric or ceramics catalog. Her paintings differ in how she modifies their self-similar but differentiated elements (slightly different triangles, variously oriented ovals, circles that change size, for example). She transforms ordinary periodic patterns by infusing their elements with historical relationships: the restless line of Klee, the stoic compositions of Mondrian, and the personality of Pollock. The results refer to none of them visually yet are clearly derived from all of them. Her paintings are simultaneously static and peripatetic (Klee), universal and specific (Mondrian), generic and personal (Pollock). Despite these misfit qualities, her sensibility is consistent.[37]

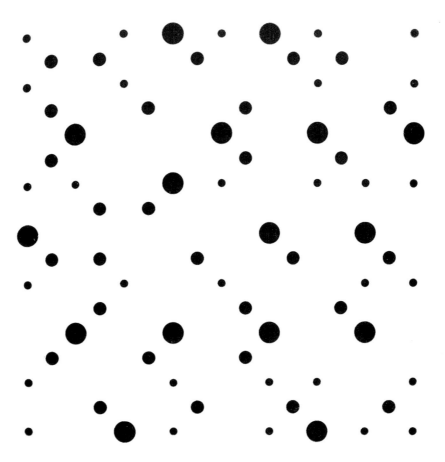

White Disks, Bridget Riley (1964). The seemingly random distribution of dots and peripatetic presence of afterimages (the white disks) is actually a highly controlled distribution of a small number of sequences along the vertical, horizontal, and diagonal axes.

While limited to abstract shapes and motifs, the painting proper is not meant to reinforce the flat surface. Nor is it to absorb or be contemplated by the viewer. Its effects are not found in the canvas proper, but in the gap between the work and its viewer. When she claims that the medium of her work is perception,[38] she is referring to the afterimages and dizziness that her paintings induce. Unlike art that means or represents something else—as an index, icon, or symbol—Riley's art does something to you. It causes viewers to temporarily lose control over their bodies. She contaminates the alleged universal qualities of the modernist surface with fleeting sensory encounters; flouting modernist painting's alleged rules by combining what should have remained separate, namely, the work and the psyche, the objective with the subjective, the empirical with the imaginary, and high art with low art.[39]

For Riley, patterns are at once the source and technique for generating these reflexive responses. Far from being inert and superficial images, they are active physical agents. As she manipulates them, she simultaneously mobilizes both types of adaptation, adaptive translation and adaptive specification.

The former is achieved by appropriating ubiquitous, everyday, and even decorative motifs to create intense kinesthetic responses; the latter by subtle adjustments to multiple elements, the sum of which yield unexpected visual qualities. For example, *White Disks*—named for the flickering afterimages that appear when staring at black dots on a white background—appears to be a random distribution of circles. Closer inspection reveals a simple diagrid structure on which the different size circles are centered. Further, a series of diagonal subgroups of small, medium, and large disks are distributed in repeated sequences; pairs of large dots march diagonally across the field; all but three rows are composed of a single dot size, and all columns contain either medium dots or a combination of small and large dots. Unpredictable sensory effects are generated by highly disciplined relationships between parts. The manipulations are not done in the name of stability, continuity, or order; nor are they simply acts of personal expression. A similarly rigorous base triangle grid in *Shift* is iteratively altered to create a pattern that visually oscillates between figure, field, and surface, also producing (Ed Ruscha's most desirable) "Huh? Wow!" response.

Shift, Bridget Riley (1963). Minimal differentiation at the local level generates perceptual effects at multiple scales. Riley used highly rationalized patterns to create powerful sensory responses in viewers.

The ambiguity of what her paintings do and how they do it creates a plasticity, which, according to Riley, "hangs between the cognitive reading of an image and its perception."[40] It is this plastic quality that gives it "sense," a way of knowing that exists between concepts and theories, facts and experience. In contrast to those who define her work as utopian, universalist, or ahistorical, Hickey sees it as a bridge between two traditionally isolated trends, serving as an "articulate precursor to the rhetorical-empirical brand of 'behaviorist modernism' practiced by Bruce Nauman and Richard Serra, for whom, as for Riley, the manipulation of material and formal means is directed toward the evocation of a local, cognitive-kinesthetic experience that is quite distinct from linguistic communication . . . and formal appreciation . . . liberates young artists from the tyranny of explanation."[41]

Far from being decadent decoration or an optical gimmick—from being politically irresponsible or aesthetically vapid—Riley's paintings rest between an inward experience and a theatrical encounter. They shift aesthetics' relationship with art, moving it from the cognitive reflection upon objects to knowledge obtained from direct sensation and the mental faculties of "recognition and empathy."[42]

Her work is felt before it is reasoned.

This ability recalls Bateson's observation that all successful art contains "skill and pattern." Skill is the ability to do things that most cannot; pattern is the means of communicating that skill (by way of redundancy and noise).[43] The capacity to deploy pattern, regardless of content, is how art articulates relationships between ideas and objects, between mind and nature. It is a form of knowledge that is distinctly different from other, more rational ones, and therefore produces a different kind of intelligence. The subconscious associations generated by interlocking circuits of art are more complex and holistic than forms of knowledge that are limited by consciousness and purpose. In other words, art—as an aesthetic process—is better able to find connections between things than science, an ability Bateson recognized was dangerously lacking in an increasingly mechanized and self-disciplining world.[44] And, he notes, patterns (visual, aural, tactile, etc.) serve as both the means and the ends to this complex, synthetic process.

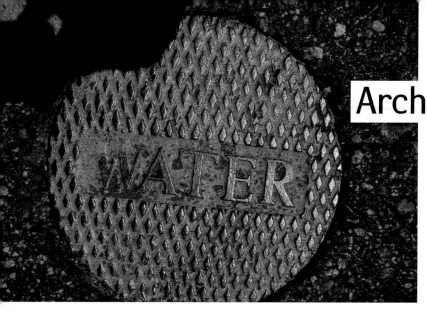

Architec+ural Varie+y

Different historical moments call for different—even counterintuitive—modes of adaptation to contest the status quo. Opening up a culture that favors ideas over sensations, concepts over materials, and a general distrust of the aesthetic (knowledge acquired by the senses) is an important consequence of effecting political, social, and cultural change via changes in sensibility. Certainly Bridget Riley's work was a reaction against this balkanized house where sensation had been all but evicted.

Looking beyond her better known work of the early and middle 1960s, one recognizes two parallel developments of difference: intense variation within a single patterned painting and within a series of paintings, and extreme variety between series.[45] This, along with her rigorous use of empirical methods, which incorporate recursive and stochastic processes to consistently produce visually stimulating patterns, reinforces how crucial aesthetic skill and intelligence are to forging connections across a diverse set of problems.

It also implies analogous ways for architecture to use patterns. Riley's ability to manipulate highly geometrical, flat surfaces to produce visceral responses is already akin to how architecture is created and experienced. For her, the disruptive yet unifying act was to employ strictly painterly techniques to convert simple graphic devices into complex physiological and psychological effects. What medium-specific processes does architecture have at its disposal to make, use, and interact with patterns? What kinds of patterns can architects use as the origin or basal condition of a project? What kinds of effects can be achieved through their manipulation? From the print on a shirt to a structural diagram, potentially any pattern can be adapted to meet architecture's many demands. The source has to be understood and represented as a pattern with aesthetic qualities, qualities that can be deployed within and between design's internal and external domains.

The use of patterns within a trajectory of modern art that includes Riley, Ross Bleckner, Casey Reas, and others, suggests the importance of variety, of cross-categorical combination, as a type of difference that can complement architects' ever-expanding command over variation. As in art, this will result from coupling intuitive working methods with advanced technology to produce carefully choreographed and wildly diverse material qualities. By promiscuously borrowing the most exotic attributes of patterns that have not traditionally been seen in architecture, it is possible to open new territories of aesthetics and logic.

David Salomon

CHAPTER 4 : PROTEAN PA++ERNS

Style is the sign of innovation, of passage into new territory.

Michel Serres

Establishing links between otherwise disparate cultural, intellectual, and technological categories has long been the job of the architect. An arbiter of aesthetic connection, who else can create a bond between the Parthenon and a sports car, bricks and B movies, octogenarians and the color orange? This task is not as esoteric as it may seem. The ability to produce relationships where none existed before is endemic to both the production and experience of architecture. The aesthetic power of patterns promotes this synthetic activity. The artistic power of patterns elevates an epistemology of making anew rather than merely uncovering the hidden; one concerned with what could be in addition to what is.

An advanced understanding of architectural patterns, one in which they merge multiple discrete interests, is particularly well suited to combine the competing formal, functional, and representational demands placed on design today. In both abstract and aesthetic manifestations, the repetition found in a pattern does not optimize or essentialize—its redundancy is a measure of its potential to absorb and respond to information, material behavior, and forces. It can incorporate multiple building systems or adapt to new requirements over time without sacrificing the performance or aesthetic agenda of any one.

Fueled by the introduction of new technologies and revised conventions of style, form, and temporality, architectural patterns remix distinct discursive and epistemological domains by anticipating unseen links between them. Advanced patterns promiscuously combine a variety of materials, performance requirements, environmental factors, sensibilities, elastic geometries, optical effects, and kinetic forces. Because they do not discriminate between scales, materials, and applications, they create connections between these aspects of architecture in a manner that is at once direct and seductive.

Combinatorial Intensity

If previous architectural conceptions of patterns limited their uses to either decorative or conceptual roles, the most sophisticated varieties today assimilate multiple functions

Purple Haze, Gnuform, MoMA PS1 (2006). Model interior. Subtle differences in the canopy's perforation pattern, materials, color, light, and water produce an ever-changing hazy atmosphere underneath.

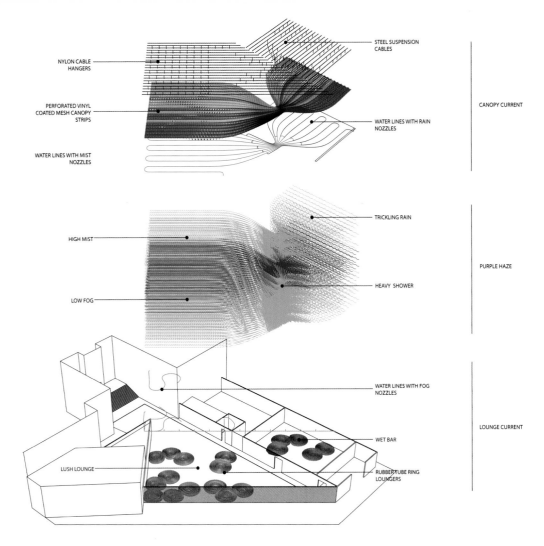

NYLON CABLE HANGERS

STEEL SUSPENSION CABLES

PERFORATED VINYL COATED MESH CANOPY STRIPS

WATER LINES WITH RAIN NOZZLES

WATER LINES WITH MIST NOZZLES

CANOPY CURRENT

HIGH MIST

TRICKLING RAIN

LOW FOG

HEAVY SHOWER

PURPLE HAZE

WATER LINES WITH FOG NOZZLES

WET BAR

LUSH LOUNGE

RUBBER TUBE RING LOUNGERS

LOUNGE CURRENT

Purple Haze. Composite axonometric. Patterns in the suspension cable system, vinyl canopy, water lines, and fog and spray nozzles asymmetrically distribute moisture, sunlight, and heat through the courtyard.

and coordinate a myriad of behaviors and effects. Even when initially developed to organize one building system, say a structural frame or curtain wall, the same pattern can absorb and respond to other information, material, or forces. A key feature of combinatorial patterns is that they are temporally multistatic—many different conditions are present at any given moment, not only in a composite pattern but also in any component within it. The excess repetition in patterns allows some parts to be active and others dormant while distributing various functional roles asymmetrically across space and time. Structural, mechanical, graphic, lighting, formal, and material components can reconfigure and even merge, occupying various channels of an over engineered diagram.

An example is *Purple Haze*, Gnuform's proposal for the MoMA/PS1 courtyard, where a number of interrelated material patterns generate zones of differing color, weather, and sensory depth. The most conventionally patterned aspects are found in the differentially perforated surface of the purple and magenta canopy that hovers above the entire space. The vinyl-covered fabric is draped from regularly spaced cables to create a wrinkled surface. Together with a series of locally specific cuts, the folds generate a complex visual pattern.

Yet Gnuform's design demonstrates that visuality is only one platform on which patterns hold strong and varied positions. The canopy pattern varies functionally and is integrated with every other component in the project. For example, some of its more clearly defined subsections correspond to the outline of the loungers located directly below. Over sporadically distributed seating in the Lush Lounge section, perforations are smaller and fewer to provide shade from sun, and mist is emitted from a high concentration of nozzles placed just beneath the canopy—the purple haze of the title forming when the mist hovers below the purple surface. The interaction between the canopy, the shimmering and rustling flaps, the mist, and the loungers creates a dynamic kinesthetic experience and vague spaces bounded by a sultry summer atmosphere. Inside the Wet Bar section things are slightly inverted, but equally complex and patterned. The water nozzles produce a steady rain and are used to softly demarcate one zone from another. The canopy above these areas has numerous lateral cuts, nearly evenly spaced, that almost completely open up to the sky. Far from being solely visual, the patterned canopy is nothing less than an active organizational device for a complex delivery of ongoing and volatile atmospheric and sensory effects—

effects that are likely to be felt as much as seen. Able to oscillate between indexical registrations, symbols of forces in flux, and sensory stimuli, a pattern is a "plateau," it is "a continuous self-vibrating region of intensities whose development avoids any orientation toward a culmination point or external end."[46] Features within it yield aftereffects that can be injected back into a pattern to generate future mutations. They offer a specific type of experience, one that is paradoxically immersive and partial but always highly sensual.

Establishing such vibes, styles, and hypersaturated sensory systems is a role particularly suited to patterns. A pattern's sensibility can be both responsive and influential; an active agent organizing material and functional forces as it elicits emotional and sensory responses. Experiments with them provide a foundation for formal and material opulence that can be driven primarily by ambiance and aesthetic intent without recourse to (yet without neglecting) structural or contextual legitimization. But even though a project's sensibility is generally believed to be loose, its elaboration relies on precisely calibrated lighting distributions, material organizations, and formal articulations to be most effectively crystallized.

Patterns vibrate—like stimulants, sedatives, and hallucinogens they affect our brains and senses with the differential dissemination of luminescence, sheen, color, heat, and texture.

Elastic Precision

Architects' proficiency in creating and manipulating form allows us to make, modify, and deploy patterns unlike those of previous generations. The selection or generation of a pattern can go a long way toward establishing a domain of sensibility. Most patterns can undergo dramatic deformations without leaving that domain, and the deformations themselves can even amplify and differentiate the desired sensibility. Formal elasticity, for example, translates to a gradient control of features and effects. Patterns, and different zones within them, can be programmed to disappear and reappear, or intensify and disperse, depending on specific temporal, social, or spatial requirements. Their repetition allows for both fine and coarse differences, from the almost imperceptible to the almost antithetical, to exist at the same time. Such differentiation can be noncomplementary. Qualitative change in one place does not have to produce compensatory change in another, evading one-to-one correlations (differences can be localized or more generally distributed, depending on the nature of the pattern and the forces inflecting it).

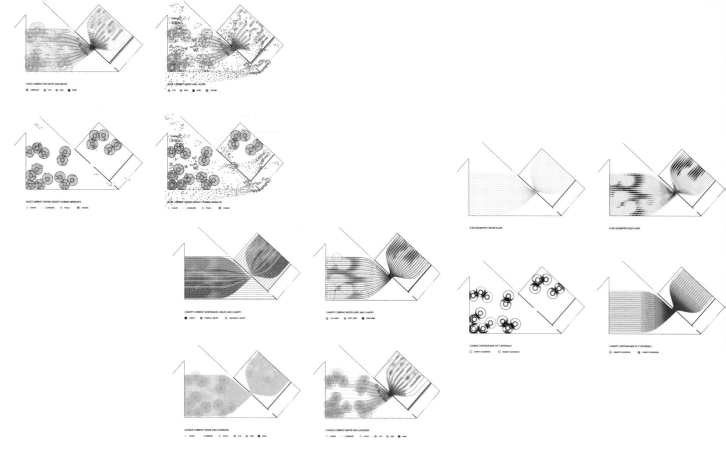

Purple Haze. Plan layers and currents. Different material systems and atmospheric effects are coordinated with the canopy geometry, water systems, dynamic crowd behavior, and the locations of rubber tube loungers.

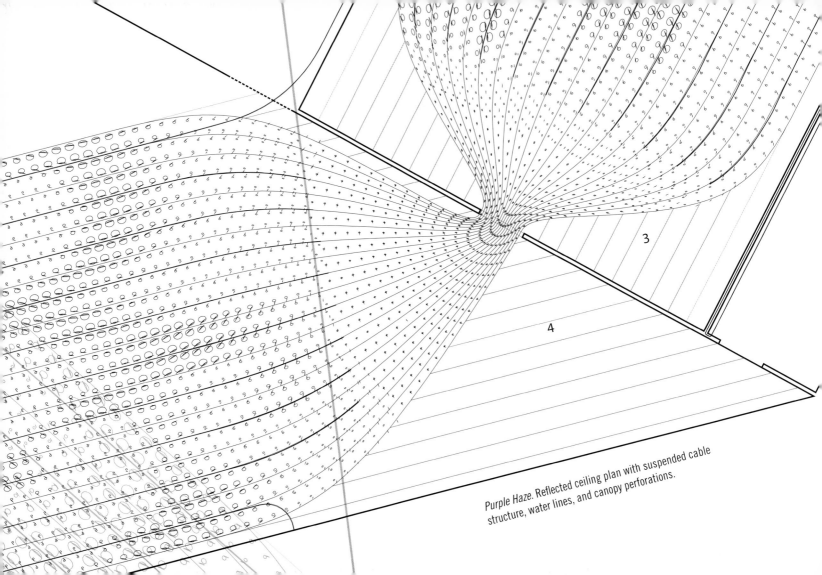

Purple Haze. Reflected ceiling plan with suspended cable structure, water lines, and canopy perforations.

3

4

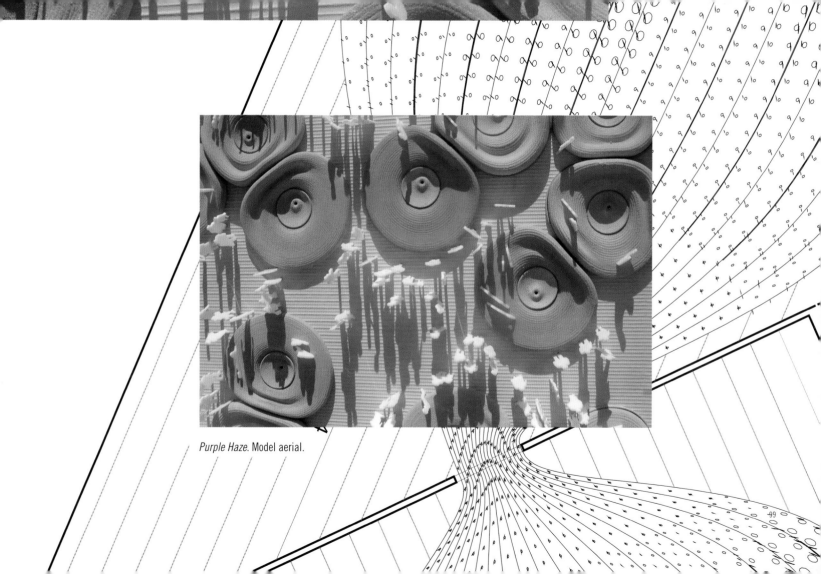

Purple Haze. Model aerial.

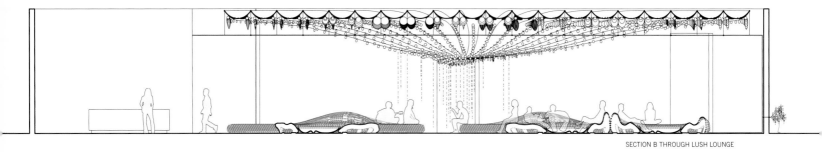

SECTION B THROUGH LUSH LOUNGE

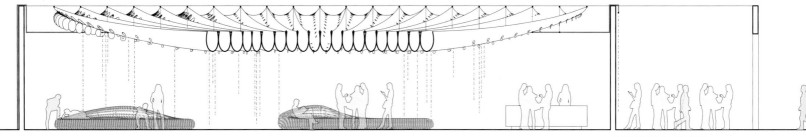

SECTION A THROUGH WET BAR

Purple Haze. Sections. Different forms of water (rain, mist, fog) and clusters of loungers create soft boundaries between variously programmed interior zones.

MLL: ☀ new kind of
wall, column, window —
not fixed but
soft & in motion
w/in its patterns
both specific
& generalized

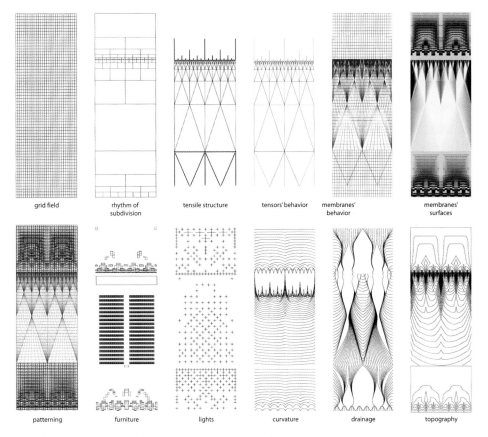

grid field	rhythm of subdivision	tensile structure	tensors' behavior	membranes' behavior	membranes' surfaces
patterning	furniture	lights	curvature	drainage	topography

Wmembrane, Ciro Najle (2005). Plan layers. From an initially simple subdivision system, subtle and unexpected formal features and material behaviors are produced.

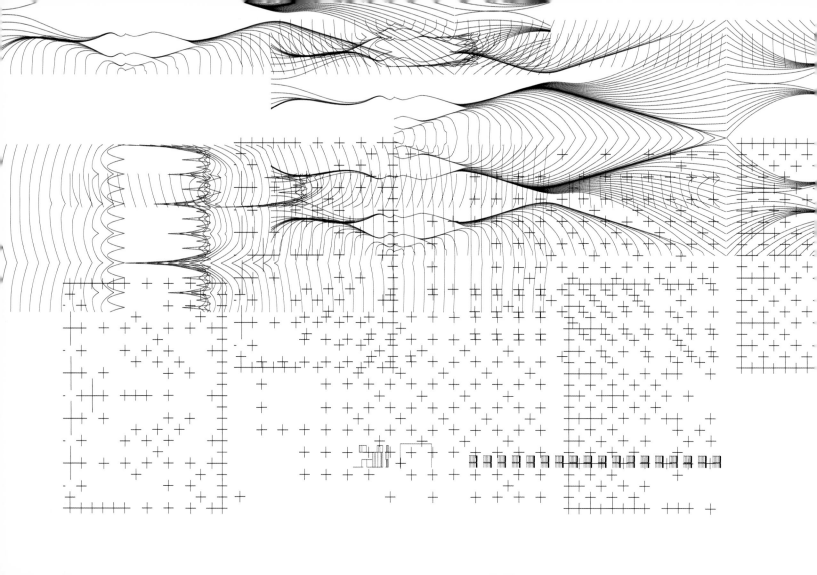

Yet, despite extensive transformative pressure, patterns maintain their visual identity. Their abstract and elastic properties enable them to determine some of a project's features without being calcified in a particular configuration. A single pattern can carry out one agenda while incorporating the constraints of others. For example, it can keep its feel and its look, even as it absorbs typological, structural, formal, and material input.

The crucial step toward an elastic identity is evident in Ciro Najle's **Wmembrane,** an amphitheater for short-term events, performances, and ceremonies. The provisional shape of the roof is the result of interactions between a tensile structure comprising vertical struts, diagonal wires, variously sized sandbags, and an overabundant quantity of fabric; the topography; and the specific sizes, locations, participants, and furniture of the events it is to house. The morphological categories present in the structure—triangular, catenary, and granular—are each clearly articulated, yet subservient to the overall aesthetic produced by their combination.

Though the catenary form of the canopy is structurally efficient, it is not solely determined by structural considerations. The many layers of the plan, geometrically coordinated and visually distinct, are inflected by topography, the circulation of various materials,

programmatic features, and unpredictable changes in the structure's environment. In heavy rain or wind the roof might sag or flutter. Forces applied to the composite system are absorbed by excess material, producing numerous discernible variations of the amphitheater over time. The very redundancy of this material gives the project a clear but dynamic identity.

Marked by billowing forms and diaphanous material in the canopy and softly sloped sand bags on grade, the amphitheater is an elaborate coalition of building systems channeled through interrelated and patterned material layers. Within any one of these layers, **individual components are scaled and positioned with local precision,** while the larger field in which they are located is graphically consistent and distinct. A close look at the overlaps of layers reveals a second order of precision: the redundancy of parts not only enables tight correspondence between components on different layers, be they material connections or mutually influential performances, but also translates to a capacity for a single pattern to perform many functions. Redundant parts of the project's plan diagrams indicate where building components are working within multiple systems (for example, where a tensile cable, a membrane surface, and a drainage channel align). By oversaturating

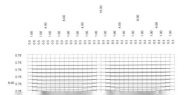

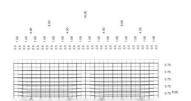

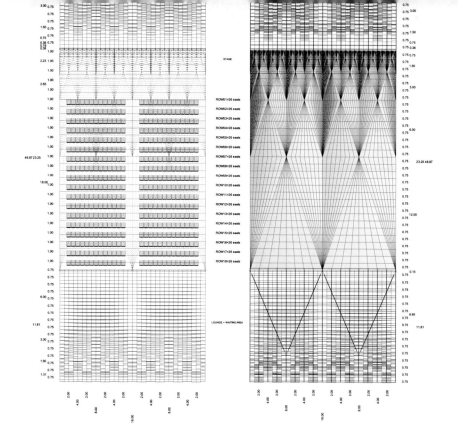

Wmembrane. Plans reveal where different systems locally align.

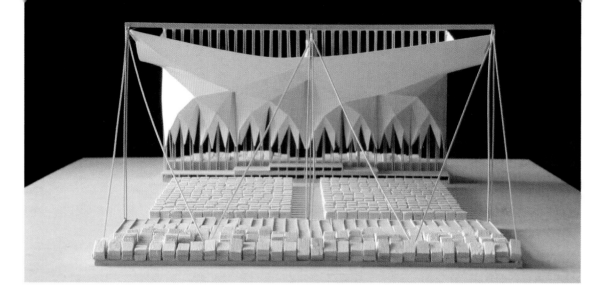

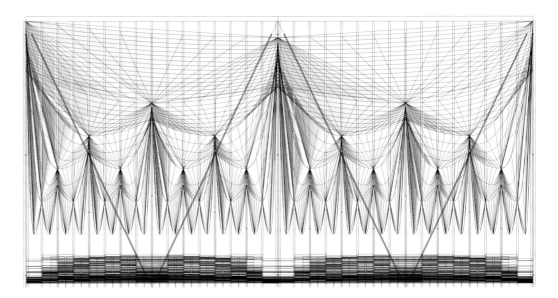

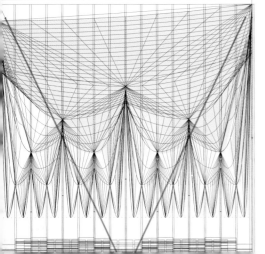

Wmembrane. Elevation. The addition of excess material to the highly rational network of tent posts and tensors produces an intricate pattern of folds that respond to changing environmental conditions.

the building with versatile and closely calibrated parts, a wide variety of forms and behaviors can be embedded.

A by-product of a highly repetitive and rule-based organization is that its constituent parts can be easily measured and adjusted, both in absolute values and relative to one another. This means that any deformation in design and construction is easily known and precise, a property of which the *Wmembrane* project takes advantage. Whether to deploy atmospheric effects, formal properties, or graphic features, or to engineer a number of material behaviors, the calculability of the pattern, its parts, and the relationships between them provides an opportunity for open and rigorous control.

In *Wmembrane* this control can be exercised at the level of the individual component, at the level of a single material system (tensile structure or fabric, for example), and at the level of composite behavior. Made possible by recent technological advances, the ability to easily and accurately coordinate multiple scales of a project allows one to combine a pattern's constituent parts in new ways— ways that are not merely additive, but create synthetic characteristics. As seen in *Wmembrane*, combinatorial patterns, in which several highly structured and even

regular systems, rhythms, or operations are overlaid, can uniquely and paradoxically yield smooth heterogeneities and irruptive anomalies (for example, idiosyncratic instances of flatness in the otherwise even transition from smooth to rough topography). This is possible because their various layers of input are repetitive but not derivative of one another. Any two layers might coincide to produce positive interference at one moment, but slip out of sync in the next. Some alignments have distinctive effects, particularly when there is a large number of coincidental layers, while misalignments generate smooth, slight changes or even homogenous noise—both qualities being visibly registered in the pattern's numerous but discrete parts.

The integration of many different layers does not always create a smooth consistency. In fact, syncopating multiple patterns often yields intermittent idiosyncrasy within a continuously differentiated assemblage. Though these idiosyncrasies may look foreign and even arbitrary within the pattern's overall composition, they are produced by repetitive operations in an organized structure. They can be replicated, diverted, or recalibrated with precision—a litmus test of the balance between the pattern's complexity and the designer's influence on it.

Developing sophisticated, new ways to deform and deploy them allows architects to create types and qualities of patterns that are utterly unlike those found in other disciplines, to be at the forefront of both aesthetic and organizational evolution. In addition to translating our most current formal organizations and systems of differentiation into advances in other fields, patterns might be the source of new theories in those fields. The agility of today's projects should not be viewed as merely the result of an intelligent design process but as an initial step toward a new intelligence. Since we are skilled at generating new patterns, why not use them to seed a synthetic knowledge of design?

Typological Promiscuity

Patterns are interchangeable in two important ways. First, one pattern can often be substituted for another without any functional let down. Second, a single pattern can switch back and forth between performing one task and another—moving seamlessly between very different scales, materials, functions, and project types. Given this fluidity, selecting a base pattern can guide a project's development in a particular direction, without limiting its potential to operate as a diagram for a number of material systems. For example, choosing a currently fashionable pattern would be an effective way to heighten a project's cultural currency. Architects are often unusually sensitive to what is most desirable in a wide range of media—clothing, music, furniture, graphics, and industrial technology, to name a few. And patterns within those genres can provide a way to translate this curatorial skill into design. Extradisciplinary sources are as viable as those with an architectural track record—a Versace print is as good as a diagrid. The difference between them is that the Versace pattern has elevated cultural relevance, the diagrid a structural relevance. Of course, a Versace print is not optimized for structural applications, so once engineered to function as such, it will contain redundancy and excess, which provide an opportunity to flood the pattern with additional functional roles. Migrating through so many types—from graphic to structural to behavioral to thermal—compounds a pattern's relevance and appeal.

Foreign Office Architect's *John Lewis Department Store* in Leicester, England, is one instance of typological promiscuity, where a lace pattern is deployed to perform multiple architectural roles. While it reflects the city's long affiliation with the textile and hosiery industries, it also functions technically, modulating light transmission and producing dynamic moiré effects in the facade. Four versions of the pattern, each with different degrees of transparency, are mapped onto the rectangular glass panels that make up the building's double-layer envelope. Although each of the four templates is unique, they align at their edges to create a seamless, complex pattern that appears non-repetitive and obscures the surface's tessellated construction. The moiré effect of the two etched glass layers not only generates an iconic image for the store, but the different degrees of transparency and reflection provide unusual visual connections between the store and the city, and provide solar protection where needed.

While FOA's pattern is a reincarnation of one of John Lewis's historic textiles, the source of Jurgen Mayer's *Mensa Moltke* building in Karlsruhe, Germany is more obscure. For the design of this college dining hall, the firm transformed a data-protection pattern found on the inside of bank envelopes into a three-dimensional structural and

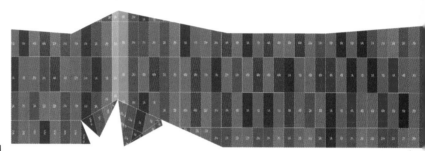

John Lewis Department Store, Foreign Office Architects, Leicester, UK (2008).

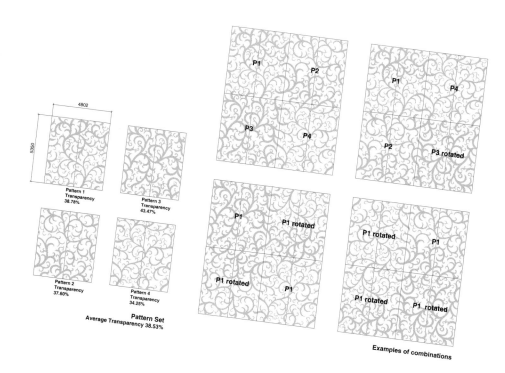

Pattern 1
Transparency
38.78%

Pattern 3
Transparency
43.47%

Pattern 2
Transparency
37.60%

Pattern 4
Transparency
34.25%

Pattern Set
Average Transparency 38.53%

P1   P2
P3   P4

P1   P4
P2   P3 rotated

P1   P1 rotated
P1 rotated   P1

P1 rotated   P1
P1 rotated   P1 rotated

Examples of combinations

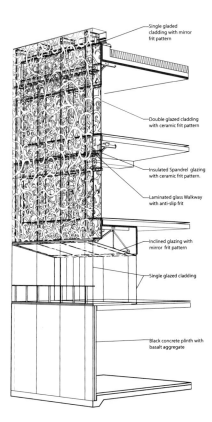

Single gladed
cladding with mirror
frit pattern

Double glazed cladding
with ceramic frit pattern

Insulated Spandrel glazing
with ceramic frit pattern.

Laminated glass Walkway
with anti-slip frit

Inclined glazing with
mirror frit pattern

Single glazed cladding

Black concrete plinth with
basalt aggregate

John Lewis Department Store. Four tiles with different
configurations and degrees of transparency seamlessly
connect to create an apparently non-repetitive pattern.

John Lewis Department Store. Envelope section.

inner layer

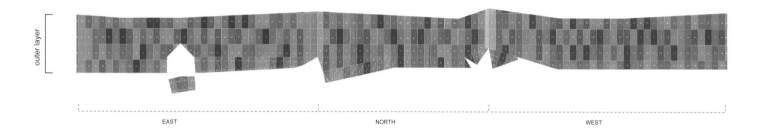

outer layer

EAST   NORTH   WEST

Patterns

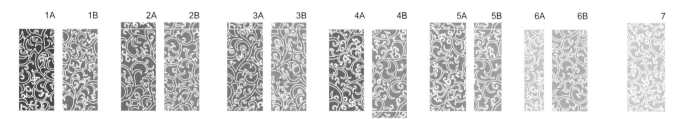

1A   1B   2A   2B   3A   3B   4A   4B   5A   5B   6A   6B   7

John Lewis Department Store. Unfolded elevation. Colors indicate the arrangement of the four tile types

spatial system. From graphic, to abstract model, to building, the pattern is ubiquitous. The intricate web generated by their multistep transformation is everywhere and everywhere distorted: in the roof plan, portico, beams, and lighting. Individual parts of the pattern are thickened and attenuated as needed to accommodate particular bearing, partitioning, and circulatory requirements. For example, the staircase to the mezzanine level is embedded in an overscaled truss. Similarly, the patterned integration of lighting into the columns and beams reinforces the spatial pattern, the two combining to create complex visual effects. It may seem eccentric to use a security envelope lining as the basis for a building's structural and spatial logic. But as a result, all of the building's parts, from rooms to columns, to windows, are integrated into a coherent aesthetic package and calibrated to function well.

In each of these projects, a pattern works in different scales, materials, and functional contexts, a capability that results from its variable repetition. Patterns are quantified, cellular, yet continuous and malleable. Even the most capricious choice of patterns—"I saw it at Urban Outfitters and I liked it" or "I got it from a bank envelope"—

can be calibrated to highly complex design criteria because of its parsed internal organization. Patterns' ease of translation not only facilitates communication with other fields but also means that architects can import unconventional patterns into their projects to expand visual diversity. And the plethora of possible patterns is multiplied by a wide range of modifications—including amplifications, distortions, erasure, blending, duplications, merging, and projections.

Evanescent Brilliance

Issues of temporality loom behind common criticisms of patterns—that they are either timeless or fleetingly trendy. Consistent with the synthetic logic by which today's patterns operate, opening up territory between these poles suggests new kinds of projects. One kind combines stable or even inert behaviors with more responsive ones—patterns that literally shift in response to stimuli. Another pushes beyond the apparent limits of the pattern's temporal spectrum to produce ultrastable and ultravolatile variants. Inextricably linked to their visual power is the proclivity for patterns to be meteoric, to be momentarily and intensely appealing, brilliant, relevant, or effective.

From graphic, to abstract model, to building, the pattern is ubiquitous

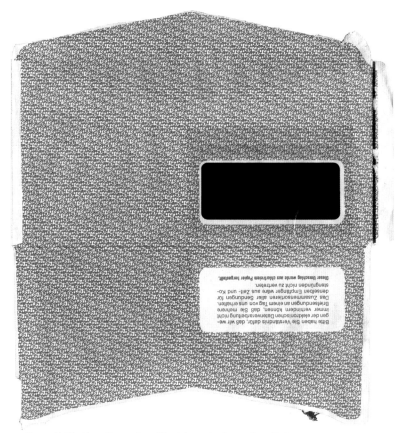

Mensa Moltke. Security envelope. The data-protection pattern that lines common bank envelopes is the source of the project's structural and spatial organization.

Mensa Moltke. Interior. The building's three-dimensional structural and spatial pattern also distributes lighting and is locally thickened to incorporate a stair.

Mensa Moltke, J. Mayer H. Architects, Karlsruhe, Germany (2007). Exterior. The portico emphasizes the pattern's potential for depth, while flush windows on the side elevations recall its graphic origin.

(opposite) *Mensa Moltke*. Model. A security envelope's graphic pattern is expanded to a three-dimensional web.

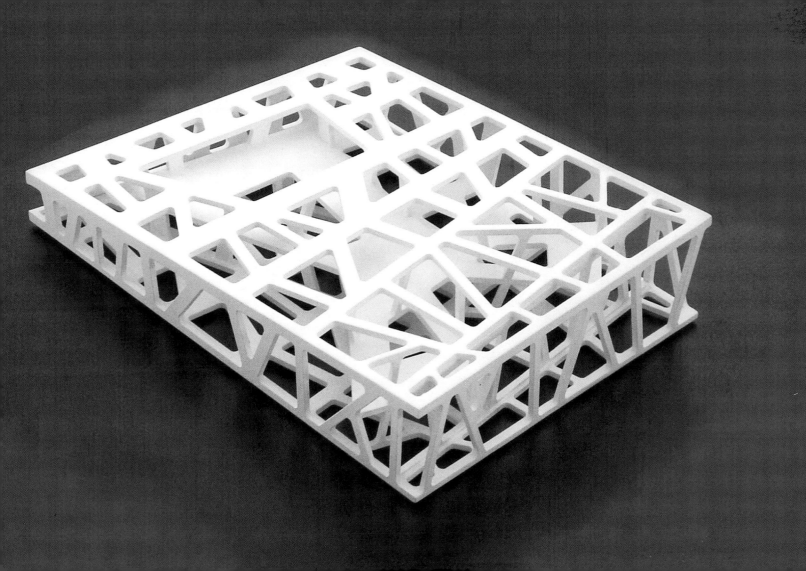

The field's long-standing emphasis on stability and timelessness as hallmarks of serious work has unnecessarily limited the scope of projects that architects are apt to target. New provisional and unstable patterns are creating dynamic geometric organizations and sensual tonalities that open the door to projects that define a cultural moment, no matter how short. A comparison of BIG's *People's Building Shanghai* and *Tivoli Retail Store,* two projects with similarly patterned facades, showcases a single pattern's ability to be deployed in both stable and fleeting ways. Circles in the *People's Building* facade are structurally driven, increasing in size on upper floors where loads are comparatively less than below. A pattern can play no more serious a role than to govern structure, particularly in a tall building. In the *Tivoli* envelope, the same circles are manifest as glowing bubbles containing items for sale—in the best tradition of Tivoli buildings of the fifties and sixties, the bubbles make the project light. Neither the building itself nor the pleasure it creates are meant to last. In fact, its success is in the bubble pattern's ability to concentrate appeal to such an extent that it soon quickly evaporates. Because it doesn't claim to have a unique essence, a single pattern can create different types and degrees of appeal over varying lengths of time.

Other projects would benefit from a similar tolerance of expendability, sometimes for more functional reasons. Many environments are defined by repetitious and variable behavior. A major challenge for architecture is to link fluctuating and patterned activity—in light, heat, data, traffic, weather, flight, migration, money, and psychological response—to corresponding material systems. In doing so, architects will design how patterns change when stimulated by their environments, and how they can stimulate those environments in turn. Material- and market-based systems are particularly useful comparisons in this regard because their patterns include both ephemeral and recurring phenomena; the volatile and the stable are always present. For example, certain graphic patterns—in clothing, society, and architecture—never seem to go out of style, while others do. This capacity to have short and long life spans disrupts architecture's obsession with longevity, balancing it out with the different durational demands of the contemporary. Within an evanescent pattern's logic of dynamism, the sudden, violent, and short-term changes associated with fashion and planned obsolescence are no longer direct challenges to architecture's cultural status. Rather, the combination of positive and negative feedback loops that feed these behaviors is isomorphic to how architecture can produce new patterns over time.

People's Building (2007) and (overleaf) *Tivoli Store* (2007), BIG. Perspective and model photo. The similarly bubbly sensibility of the office building and gift shop challenges any claims to structural seriousness, scalar propriety, or the ethics of typological expression. Instead, they exhibit a pattern's potential for evanescent appeal and promiscuously migrating between different project types and scales.

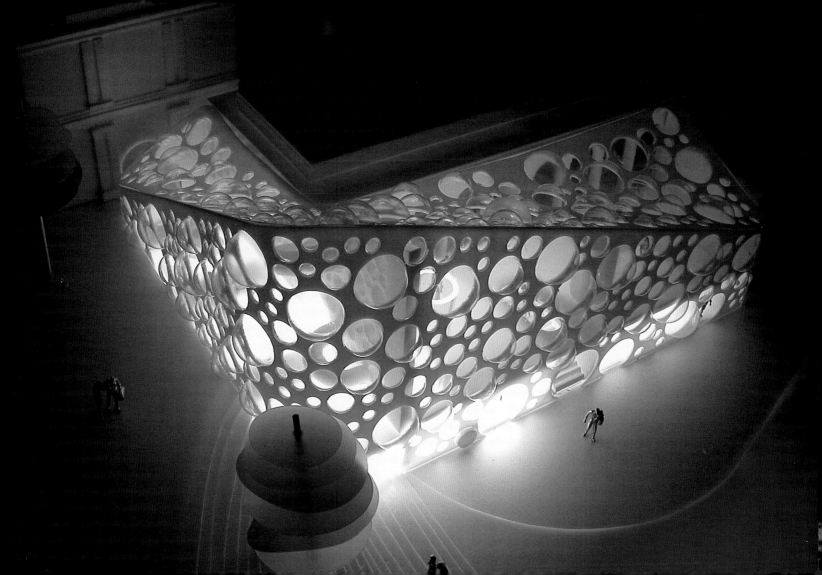

Adapting patterns to fluctuating desires and contingencies can be an ongoing process, with design becoming a method of directing change in patterns, a way of guiding them through different configurations. This relies on making and using patterns that are more responsive than their modernist predecessors.

is this really true? what about acoustic, olfactory etc.

Visual Coherence

Today's patterns are first and foremost visual ones, which can provide a project with aesthetic clarity despite differences in individual components, the complex structure of relationships between components, and even shifts between foreground and background. Visual attributes are always present and recognizable, so a base pattern's identity remains separate yet linked to the forces that shape it. Because of its internal consistency, a pattern produces gestalts that allow one to recognize and understand otherwise overwhelmingly complex designs. As both diagrams and design motifs, patterns are unique in how they blend things (obfuscation by repetition) and how they distinguish things (by both borders and changes in intensity). The production and modification of redundant parts—which have the capacity to visually combine foreground with background—is key. Of course, architectural discourse has been obsessed with the distinction between foreground and background or, more specifically, with figures and grounds. Typically, a singular image or space allows for multiple readings, depending on the focus and position of the subject observing them. However, only one reading is present, or foregrounded, at a time. One can perceptually oscillate between one figure and another, but never are the two readings present. It's either on or off. Ambiguity is produced and understood compositionally and thus only is experienced optically.

Patterns advance and undermine the relationship between figure and ground, as they have the capacity to simultaneously blur, reveal, gradate, and accentuate distinctions between object and atmosphere by repetition and extension. Both conceptually and graphically they can be reproduced an infinite number of times. A swatch of fabric, a roll of fencing, a strand of chain, a sheet of metal grating are not "essentialist" or even gestalt systems but support the emergence and recession of a pattern's visual identity. In this way patterns are not linear, totalizing, or teleological, as they are never complete.

Emergent's *Novosibirsk Summer Pavilion* illustrates the pattern's ability to be both foregrounded and backgrounded. Panels that form the building's envelope adhere to different geometric principles at different scales: its surface is first subdivided into nearly planar polygons with varying numbers of sides, and those panels are in turn subdivided into a patchwork of four-sided polygons that locally control weight and stiffness. Different sizes and materials render clusters of panels visually strong in some places and far more subtle in others. A similar pattern in the paving of the plaza in which the building is sited creates a parallel range of explicit and blended readings: it is alternatively a distinct object and part of a larger field. In all of the pattern's various states, what is generated according to a structural logic becomes primarily and dynamically visual.

On one hand, patterns' all-over surface presence can act to camouflage the objects with which they are integrated and the components or rules from which they are made. On the other, many graphic patterns stand out from their contexts when intense, whimsical, and bold. The former is akin to the total environments exemplified in many Art Nouveau interiors. It is also reminiscent of the equally overwhelming system of patterns developed by Christopher Alexander. The latter conforms to a more traditional definition of ornament, as something added on to an otherwise complete object. When they are robustly designed and imaginatively deployed, it is hard to make such distinctions in the protean patterns of today.

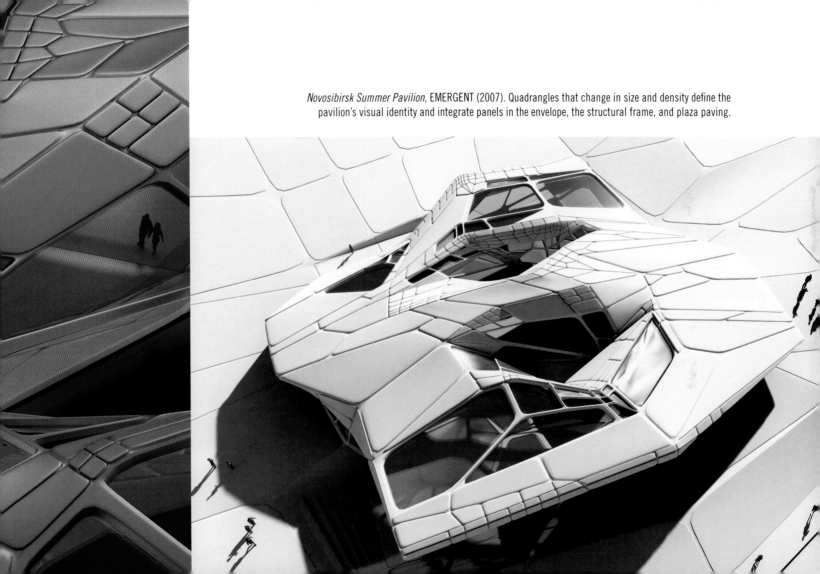

Novosibirsk Summer Pavilion, EMERGENT (2007). Quadrangles that change in size and density define the pavilion's visual identity and integrate panels in the envelope, the structural frame, and plaza paving.

Thermographic Theater, !ndie architecture (2007). Interior. A highly articulated pattern is generated by locally adjusting the density and output of a hydronic heating system.

Synaptic Intelligence

Given their functional variety, typological diversity, and redundant organization, **patterns enable architects to link otherwise incompatible fields to breed novelty and variety.** They are able to pioneer new territory in several types of architectural interstices: as synthetic diagrams, they catalyze connections between heterogeneous domains of a project; via high-resolution multiplicity, they form gradients between binary oppositions; and by way of synaptic adjacencies, they charge relationships between typically discordant material systems.

For example, flowers and real estate developments can be linked by color patterns: floral coloration is specific to form, while in suburban residential projects it is not. Introducing floral coloring to residential design would increase variation: two houses with the same color palette and differing morphology would have varying coloring schemes. Within a single house and across a neighborhood, new and diverse color patterns could be spawned. Similarly, color and climate can be linked by graphic patterns. A single graphic pattern can govern color distribution and also the organization of mechanical systems, which in turn generate various climatic conditions. And dynamic conditions of heat, light, and humidity can be coordinated with

changing color and textural fields to create sophisticated atmospheres because patterned relationships between a project's various material and mechanical systems can be organized synaptically—as a network of infinitesimal gaps across which information can be exchanged.

Synaptic methods of directing pattern changes are particularly effective when the relevant patterns exist in different media. Many patterns are materially incompatible; that is, one cannot be easily translated into another. An example can be found in retail design, where it is often necessary to coordinate store layouts (material patterns) with recognizable patterns of consumer behavior. Such environments have to be designed to actively and often inconspicuously exchange information with the shoppers that inhabit them. The way that merchandise is organized, lighting controlled, and circulation directed in relation to the movement and perception of shoppers is rarely evident but always crucial to the store's success. It turns out that repetition is key to developing relationships between the store's

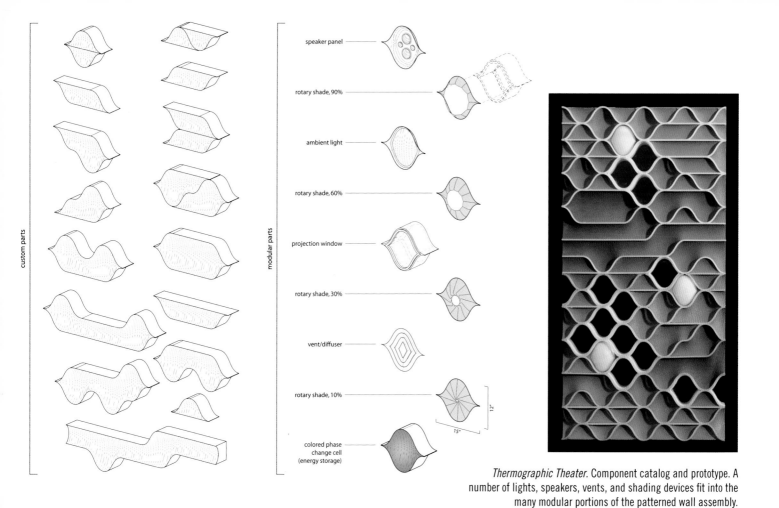

custom parts

modular parts

speaker panel

rotary shade, 90%

ambient light

rotary shade, 60%

projection window

rotary shade, 30%

vent/diffuser

rotary shade, 10%

12"

15"

colored phase
change cell
(energy storage)

Thermographic Theater. Component catalog and prototype. A
number of lights, speakers, vents, and shading devices fit into the
many modular portions of the patterned wall assembly.

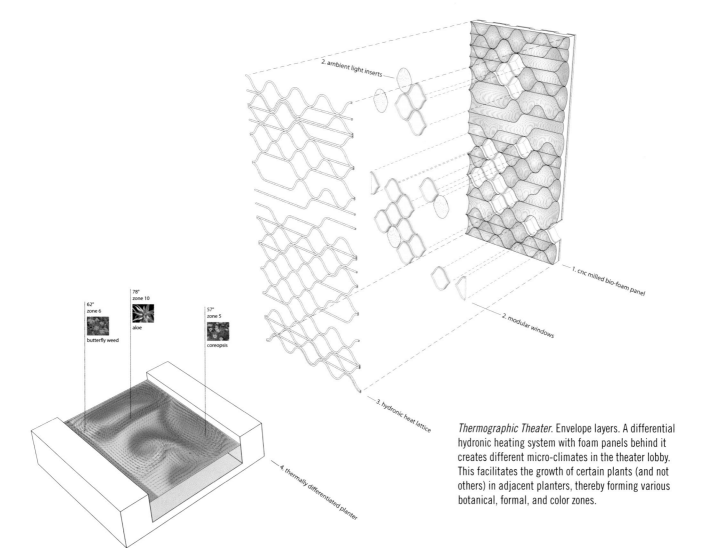

2. ambient light inserts

1. cnc milled bio-foam panel

2. modular windows

3. hydronic heat lattice

4. thermally differentiated planter

62°
zone 6

butterfly weed

78°
zone 10

aloe

57°
zone 5

coreopsis

Thermographic Theater. Envelope layers. A differential hydronic heating system with foam panels behind it creates different micro-climates in the theater lobby. This facilitates the growth of certain plants (and not others) in adjacent planters, thereby forming various botanical, formal, and color zones.

design and the responses it elicits. Envirosell, Paco Underhill's behavioral consulting firm, rigorously analyzes consumer behavior to determine how shoppers make decisions, often with an emphasis on how they are influenced by a store's layout, display strategies, and other physical features. While it is difficult to anticipate what any one shopper will do, Envirosell can determine how a given distribution of display racks and circulation corridors generates particular decision-making patterns. In the absence of predictable one-to-one relationships, Envirosell identifies tendencies in repetitious behavior and analyzes how various environmental factors drive those tendencies. Likewise, an architect cannot know how a specific design decision will affect one person's choices, but can forecast its influence on a recurring pattern of decisions or even the appearance of new patterns. As Gregory Bateson points out, redundant events beget prediction, which in turn prepares one to learn when the unexpected occurs.

predictive architecture

Informed by connections between behavioral trends and environmental features, patterns are generated and feedback loops established. Patterns in a store's

material design and in consumer responses are not permanent, stable, consistent, ideal, and standard but temporary, volatile, uneven, specific, and variable. Future patterns can build on the analysis of these qualities and demand that they be given a brand identity—one which is based upon, but not purely indexical of, the actions and reactions that produce them. In retail design, the physical environment has to be designed to actively exchange information with shoppers; it cannot merely index their decisions. When this is done, the resultant patterns not only reveal the forces acting on that environment, they also redistribute and coordinate those forces to unfold alternative environments and corresponding behaviors.

This style of pattern management—linking ones that exist in seemingly incompatible media—depends on an operative or conceptual adjacency, a microgap across which two patterns can influence one another while maintaining a subtle but important boundary between them. A project might bridge a number of observable patterns that don't register materially and ones that do. By controlling relationships in proximate formal-material patterns, a designer can adjust the probability that a particular pattern of behavior will emerge without guaranteeing its absolute and permanent existence.

The logic of linking formal and material patterns to dynamic behaviors works in non retail contexts as well. In the project titled *Thermographic Theater*—a speculative design for a movie theater complex and accompanying lounges, bookstore, and hydroponic gardens—the firm !ndie architecture uses patterns to link material, organizational, and behavioral domains. The project's backbone is a differential hydronic heat system that integrates visual, thermal, and botanical zones with circulatory systems, retail strategies, and shifting qualities of luminescence, color, and sheen. By introducing varying densities of corrugation into the standard zigzag pattern of radiant heat piping, a non-uniform version is made and asymmetrically distributed across interior wall and ceiling surfaces. It includes three interwoven pipe circuits (two hot and one cold) that can be activated in seven different combinations (and also reversed to mediate exterior temperature swings).

The hydronic pipe lattice controls changing thermal patterns in the adjacent lobby areas, which contain cafes and lounges populated with waist-high planters, retail displays, and long tables. The microclimates that the lattice forms yield diverse botanical zones, which crisscross the planters. The tables—too large for any single group to take over—are inlaid with opulent material patterns and spot lit to create soft boundaries of light that correspond to the thermal ones. Airbrushed rigid foam insulation panels are formally, texturally, and chromatically fit to the variegated pattern of the hydronic lattice. While providing an efficient backstop to the pipe system, the panels also create a number of visual tones at the interior. In all, patterns in copper tubing, heat, plants, and the form and color of the walls are integrated. By taking advantage of their capacities for incorporating multiple project domains, producing local elasticity with global consistency, synaptically linking phenomena in different media, and molding various sensory fields, the project merges custom paint jobs and microclimate engineering, form and hydroponics, furniture and consumer behavior, and a number of other heterogeneous combinations.

thermal plan a

heating circuit a

Thermal/temperature zones → mul: BIO-ZONES?

Thermographic Theater. Thermal plans. By activating different combinations of three parallel hydronic circuits—two hot and one cold— different distributions of heat can be generated at the 3' height of the planters. Cross-referencing these conditions with the USDA's Plant Hardiness Zones allows for diverse botanical landscapes to be precisely located in lounge and cafe areas between the theaters.

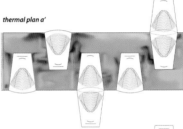

thermal plan a'

cooling circuit a'

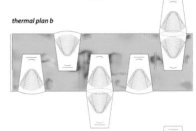

thermal plan b

heating circuit b

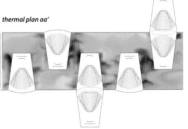

thermal plan aa'

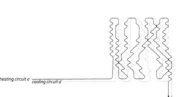

heating circuit a   cooling circuit a'

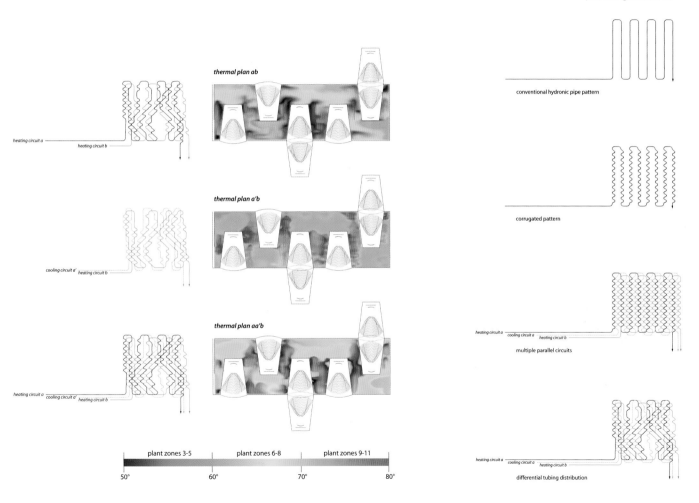

pattern generation

thermal plan ab

heating circuit a

heating circuit b

thermal plan a'b

cooling circuit a'   *heating circuit b*

thermal plan aa'b

heating circuit a
cooling circuit a'   *heating circuit b*

plant zones 3-5   plant zones 6-8   plant zones 9-11

50°   60°   70°   80°

conventional hydronic pipe pattern

corrugated pattern

heating circuit a
cooling circuit a'   *heating circuit b*

multiple parallel circuits

heating circuit a
cooling circuit a'   *heating circuit b*

differential tubing distribution

The project's syncing of material, formal, and color systems with thermal and behavioral ones echoes chemist Ilya Prigogine's uses of "pattern" to describe dissipative structures; it is hard to know if he is referring to the pattern we see or a pattern of fundamental operations behind the visible one. His theory highlights the productively tenuous connection between less visible patterns and perceptual ones. Similarly, architectural patterns needn't always be accurate indices of morphogenetic processes or associated functions. Freeing the pattern of its responsibility to express a deeper truth about how a project works while still allowing it to engage those operative aspects means that its outward appearance can opportunistically coincide with and diverge from its organizational diagram. This disparity can result in a more expansive visual palette and a concomitantly diverse body of potential functional organizations.

So although a pattern can be generated by the functional demands it has to meet, its relationship to those requirements is not an ethical one; they are not necessarily the natural or true substance of design. The polytypic nature of architectural patterns suggests that there can be a gap between the way they look and perform. A pattern can play multiple interrelated roles, each capable of being understood without knowledge or appreciation of the others. It can also appeal to multiple audiences. One might zero in on a particular coloring effect while another gravitates toward its structural logic.

— Patterns can...

Despite their ubiquitous presence, there is still widespread suspicion of patterns: on one hand, for being shallow and fleetingly popular—incapable of deep or durable influence; on the other, for being too deterministic and absolute—unable to respond to environmental changes or yield to other organizational models. Further fueling these overly conservative critiques is a generally uncritical use of patterns in design. Rarely is their deployment rigorous; seldom can a designer explain how one pattern is more effective, relevant, or better suited to a project than others.

While these tendencies might suggest that architects avoid patterns altogether, we prefer to expand and empower them via an alternative, precise, and open redefinition.

The emerging properties of today's patterns—
their ability to indiscriminately take on
functions, shift between wildly divergent scales
and types of media, maintain clear aesthetic
identities, and foster technical precision—
collectively point the way to synthetic design.
Patterns' odd combination of promiscuity and
coherence can channel architects' proficiency
in linking seemingly disparate cultural,
material, and epistemological categories.
The conflicts that they foreground—for
example, between architecture's predilection
for structural order and its fascination with
sensory affection, or its dual emphasis
on formal invention and environmental
control—are central to contemporary
practice and discourse. By reconfiguring
these debates, patterns offer numerous new
directions of evolution and, ultimately, the
possibility of producing new architecture.

closing argument

notes

1. See Reyner Banham, "Conclusion: Functionalism and Technology," *Theory and Design in the First Machine Age* (New York: Praeger, 1962), 320–330.
2. Herbert Simon, *The Sciences of the Artificial* (Cambridge: MIT Press, 1996), 1.
3. Gyorgy Kepes, *The New Landscape in Art and Science* (Chicago: P. Theobald, 1956), 206.
4. Ibid., 205.
5. Reinhold Martin, *The Organizational Complex* (Cambridge, MA: MIT Press, 2003), 40.
6. Kepes, 207.
7. For an explanation of dissipative structures, see J. Dowling, E. Curran, R. Cunningham, and V. Cahill, "Using Feedback in Collaborative Reinforcement Learning to Adapt and Optimise Decentralised Distributed Systems," *IEEE Transactions on Systems, Man and Cybernetics (Part A), Special Issue on Engineering Self-Orangized Distributed Systems*, 35, no. 3 (2005): 360–72.
8. Philip W. Anderson and Daniel L. Stein, "Broken Symmetry, Emergent Properties, Dissipative Structures, Life: Are They Related?" *Self-Organizing Systems: The Emergence of Order*, ed. F. Eugene Yates (New York: Plenum Press, 1987), 445–57.
9. Gregory Bateson, *Mind and Nature: A Necessary Unity* (New York: Dutton, 1979), 8.
10. Ibid., 13.
11. Gregory Bateson, *Steps To an Ecology of Mind* (New York: Ballantine, 1972), 416.
12. Ibid., 406.
13. Bateson, *Mind and Nature*, 46.
14. Ibid., 47.
15. Christopher Alexander, *The Timeless Way of Building* (New York: Oxford University Press), 365.
16. Gregory Bateson, *Steps To an Ecology of Mind*, 413.
17. Ibid., 147.
18. See, for example, Alejandro Zaerlo-Polo and Farshid Moussavi, "Phylogenesis: Foa's Ark," in *Phylogenesis: FOA's Ark* (Barcelona: Actar, 2004), 6–19.
19. Anthony Vidler, "Architecture's Expanded Field," *Artforum* 42 (April 2004): 142–47.
20. Gregory Bateson, *Mind and Nature*, 47.
21. A. C. Wilson and others, "Mitochondrial DNA and two perspectives on evolutionary genetics," *Biological Journal of the Linnean Society* (1985) 26, 375–400.
22. Herbert Simon, *The Sciences of the Artificial* (Cambridge: MIT Press, 1969), xi.
23. Thomas H. Beeby, "The Grammar of Ornament/Ornament as Grammar," *VIA* III (1977): 10–29.
24. See Raymond Williams, "Culture," in *Keywords: A Vocabulary for Culture and Society* (New York: Oxford University Press, 1976), for the changing definitions of culture.
25. Dave Hickey, *Beau Monde: Toward a Redeemed Cosmopolitanism* (Santa Fe: SITE, 2001), 74.
26. See Dorothy K. Washburn and Donald W. Crowe, eds., *Symmetry Comes of Age: The Role of Pattern in Culture* (Seattle: University of Washington Press, 2004).

27. E.M. Franquemont and C.R. Franquemont, "Structure of the World through Cloth," in *Symmetry Comes of Age: The Role of Pattern in Culture*, ed. Dorothy K. Washburn and Donald W. Crowe.

28. See Colin Rowe "The Chicago Frame," in *The Mathematics of the Ideal Villa and other Essays* (Cambridge: MIT Press, 1976), 89–118.

29. Rosalind Krauss, *The Optical Unconscious* (Cambridge: MIT Press, 1993); "The Grid, the /Cloud/, and the Detail," in *The Presence of Mies*, ed. Detlef Mertins (New York: Princeton Architectural Press, 1994), 110–25.

30. Arthur Loeb, "The Architecture of Crystals," in *Module, Proportion, Symmetry, Rhythm*, ed. Gyorgy Kepes (New York: George Braziller, 1966), 38–63; "Structure and Patterns in Art and Science," *Leonardo* 4 (1971): 339–46. For Kepes's own definition of patterns, see Gyorgy Kepes, "Thing, Structure, Pattern, Process," and "Transformation, Physical, Perceptual, Symbolic," in *The New Landscape in Art and Science* (Chicago: Paul Thebold, 1956), 204–07 and 226–31.

31. Gregory Bateson, *Mind and Nature*, 46–47.

32. For a summary analysis of these efforts, led by Gyorgy Kepes at MIT, see Reinhold Martin, *Organizational Complex*.

33. For a synopsis of this reception, see Pamela Lee, "Bridget Riley's Eye/ Body Problem," in *Chronophobia: On Time and Art of the 1960s* (Cambridge: MIT Press, 2004), 154–214; Frances Follin, *Embodied Visions: Bridget Riley, Op Art and the Sixties* (London: Thames & Hudson, 2004).

34. See Gregory Bateson, *Steps To an Ecology of Mind*, 454–471.

35. Bridget Riley, *The Eye's Mind: Collected Writings 1965-1999*, ed. Robert Kudielka (London: Thames & Hudson, 1999); Follin, *Embodied Visions*.

36. Dave Hickey, *Beau Monde: Toward a Redeemed Cosmopolitanism* (Santa Fe: Site, 2001).

37. See Dave Hickey, "Bridget Riley for Americans," in *Bridget Riley: Paintings 1982-2000 and Early Works on Paper* (New York: PaceWildenstein, 2000), 5–9.

38. Bridget Riley, "Perception is the Medium," *Art News* 64, no. 6 (October 1965): 32–33, reprinted in *The Eye's Mind*.

39. In Michael Freed's "Art and Objecthood", *Artforum* 5 (June 1967): 12–23, the differences between modernist and minimalist art is made along these lines.

40. Riley, "Perception is the Medium."

41. Hickey, "Bridget Riley for Americans."

42. Bateson, *Mind and Nature*, 7–11.

43. Gregory Bateson, *Steps To an Ecology of Mind*, 128–152.

44. Ibid.

45. See Hickey, "Bridget Riley for Americans," for an analysis of how this consistency is achieved.

46. Gilles Deleuze and Felix Guattari, *A Thousand Plateaus* (Minneapolis: University of Minnesota Press, 1987), 22.

illustration credits

Jina Kim, 2, 6–7, 134–5, 140–1
Paul Andersen and David Carson, 8
Paul Andersen and Sangwook Park, 11–12
Nike *Waffle Sole* and *Air Max 360 II Sole*, Paul Andersen, 15
David Carson, 16, 17, 18, 19, 49, 57, 59, 61, 62, 63, 64, 78, 87, 88, 133, courtesy of David Carson, all rights reserved.
Swiss Re Building, Sir Norman Foster and Associates, 20
Seattle Central Library, Office for Metropolitan Architecture, 21, 23
Prada Aoyama, Naoki Sugibayashi (Noisy Paradise), 21; Herzog and de Meuron, 24, 25
0-14 Tower, Reiser + Umemoto, 26, 27, 28, 29, 30, 31, 32
Clad Cuts Dress, Atelier Manferdini, 33
Nike Air Scale, Atelier Manferdini, 34
Fiori d'arancio Trays, Atelier Manferdini, 34
Guiyang Tower, Atelier Manferdini, 34
Terminal Life, Responsive Systems Group, 35, 36, 37, 39, 40
Owen Jones, *Design for Tiles*, Victoria and Albert Museum, 43, 44
Christopher Alexander, *A Pattern Language*, (London: Oxford University Press, 1977); courtesy of Oxford University Press; 44
Ghazal Abbasy Asbagh, 45–46
Gyorgy Kepes, *New Landscape in Art and Science*, (Chicago: P.Theobald, 1963); 47
Milton Van Dyke, *Benard Convection Cells*, from *An Album of Fluid Motion* (Parabolic Press, 1982); courtesy of Ms. Milton Van Dyke; 50, 51
Belousov-Zhabotinsky Reactons, Juraj Lipscher, 52–54
Lawrence Siu, 55

Hilary Pinnington, 66
Map of Human Genetic Migration, *National Geographic Magazine* 84 (March 2006): 64–65; 70, 72
Chincero Blanket (photo), Lauren Weinhold (LollyKnit), 75
Chincero Weavers at the Loom (photo), *Symmetry Comes of Age* (Seattle: Seattle University Press, 2004), 75
Diagrams of Chincero Textiles, *Symmetry Comes of Age* (Seattle: Seattle University Press, 2004), 77
Seven one-dimensional and seventeen two-dimensional symmetrical patterns, *Symmetry Comes of Age* (Seattle: Seattle University Press, 2004), 80
White Disks, © Bridget Riley 2008. All rights reserved. Courtesy Karsten Schubert London, 83
Shift, © Bridget Riley 2008. All rights reserved. Courtesy Karsten Schubert London, 85
Purple Haze, Gnuform (Jason Payne and Heather Roberge), 93, 94, 97, 98, 99, 100
Wmembrane, Ciro Najle, 101, 102, 103, 104, 105, 106–107
John Lewis Department Store, Foreign Office Architects, 108–109, 112, 113; Satoru Mishima, 110; Valerie Bennett, 111
Mensa Molke, J Mayer H Architects, 115, 117; David Franck, 116
People's Building, Bjarke Ingles Group (BIG), 119
Tivoli Store, Bjarke Ingles Group (BIG), 120
Novosibirsk Summer Pavilion, Emergent Architecture, 122, 123
Thermographic Theater, !ndie architecture, 124, 125, 126, 127, 128, 129, 130, 131

acknowledgments

Generous financial support for the book was provided by Cornell's College of Art Architecture and Planning and by a grant from the Graham Foundation.

This project began with an innocent question after a Cornell lecture and a subsequently intense discussion about patterns. Thanks to Nasrine Seraji for bringing us together there and for being the first critic and supporter of our collaboration. We owe much of the development of the ideas in this book to Ciro Najle and Sanford Kwinter, who gave us feedback throughout the writing, design, and publishing processes. Their intellectual curiosity is something to which we should all aspire. David Carson's immediate and enthusiastic response to the project provided encouragement at a most important moment. We are also grateful for the advice of our colleagues at Cornell, Harvard, and Syracuse, who took the time to challenge and promote our work on patterns. And the energy, questions, and work of our studio and seminar students helped us to sharpen and expand the scope of our own research and speculation. Thanks to Nancy Green for piloting us through our initial publication process.

This book and the events, exhibitions, and discussions that have surrounded it, would not have been possible without the encouragement, support, and guidance of Mohsen Mostafavi. Our most sincere thanks.

To Wendy, Olivia, Ben, and Emma, your patience, understanding, and love permeate the pages and patterns included here; thank you for your unwavering support and generosity.

To Ryan, Noah, Scott, and Quinn, your power of imagination is beautiful. The inquisitive and improvisational culture of our everyday life is my greatest pleasure. Always a wild ride . . .

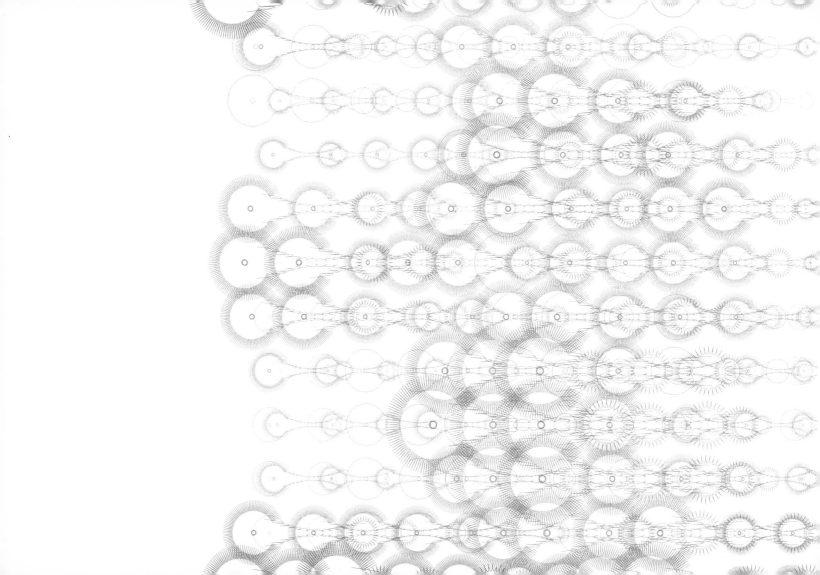

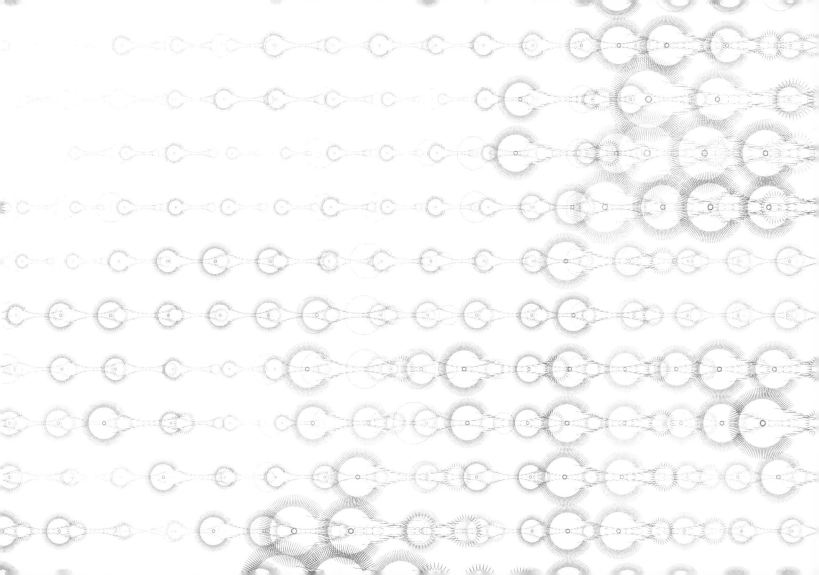

index